Chris —

Thank you for your strength and willingness to confront issues and change. Tell the truth! Keep up the good work. And remain on the "right" side of history.

THE *EMERSON* STREET STORY:

RACE, CLASS, QUALITY OF LIFE AND FAITH

In Business, Money, Politics, School, and More

JOHNNY E. BROWN

authorHOUSE®

AuthorHouse™
1663 Liberty Drive
Bloomington, IN 47403
www.authorhouse.com
Phone: 833-262-8899

Published by AuthorHouse 08/17/2020

ISBN: 978-1-7283-7080-4 (sc)
ISBN: 978-1-7283-7078-1 (hc)
ISBN: 978-1-7283-7079-8 (e)

Library of Congress Control Number: 2020915702

Print information available on the last page.

Thank you very much to the editing team, led by Carolyn J. Brown and supported by Joan Mathis, Robin Ruegg, and Dr. Abbe Boring. I am also extremely grateful to Reesha Johnette Brown Edwards for designing the book cover and photograph pages and to Mary Brown Ruegg for designing the WAPP logo and graphics.

PRAISE COMMENTS

The Emerson Street Story: Raise, Class, Quality of Life and Faith

Fresh, provocative, captivating and insightful. A masterful job of weaving together insights on race, class, quality of life, faith and more. Dr. Brown's reflections provide a fresh outlook and guide for leaders everywhere. A compelling and vital read that makes a uniquely important contribution. A truly great book.

   --Dr. Abbe Boring, former superintendent and college professor

The author's brilliant, inspiring retelling of his real life story engages you significantly in learning about him as a person who has used his experiences to build a legacy of love, strong family values, and excellence in leadership. What he shares in his autobiography serves as a foundation upon which others can create their own legacies.

   --Carolyn J. Brown, former principal and curriculum specialist

In the midst of many societal challenges, Johnny Brown deepens one's belief that close family ties are significant in shaping the social, spiritual, financial, and moral values of our lives. The illustrations in his book of systemic racism create within us a sincere desire to dispel this societal ill. A calming, yet convincing presentation.

   --Joan Mathis, high school and college instructor

Dr. Brown educates us through his stories of resilience and overcoming obstacles. A must-read for anyone wanting to learn to succeed and win in life.

   --Robin Ruegg, retired senior manager U.S. Department of the Treasury and author of *And the Home of the Braves!*

Contents

Contents

Acknowledgements

I am delighted and honored to acknowledge the contributions of many colleagues, authors, family members, and friends who helped to guide my thoughts and influenced this project from start to finish. Some have gone on to "glory" and are no longer with us in a physical sense but continue to impact my views. The list is not exhaustive. The book is intended to serve as a reflection of many who have helped in shaping how I think and write. For example, professors and authors: Drs. Asa Hilliard, Linda Darling-Hammond, Sara Lawrence-Lightfoot, Lisa Delpit, Phillip Schlechty, Nolan Estes, I. Carl Candoli, Jay D. Scribner, Michael P. Thomas, Jr., Lonnie H. Wagstaff, Walter E. Jordan-Davis, Tyrone Tanner, Manuel Justiz, Michael Fullan, John P. Kotter, Tony Wagner, Ted Dintersmith, Elvis Arterbury, Robert Nicks, Jimmy Creel, Joyce E. King, Gloria Ladsen-Billings, John I. Goodlad, Timothy J. McMannon, Larry E. Frase, Fenwick W. English, William K. Poston, Roderick Paige, Thomas L. Friedman, Patrick J. Finn, Jim Collins, Jonathan Kozol, Joyce Epstein, Howard Gardner, Stephen R. Covey, Ken Blanchard, Terry Waghorn, Jeannie Oakes, Carol A. Tomlinson, Bill Daggett, Mike Schmoker, Doug Lemov, Robert J. Marzano, W. G. Ouchi, Ivory Toldson, and Daniel Stufflebeam. Also, I am grateful for the support of my colleagues: faculties and staff of Lamar University and The University of Texas at Austin, Reverend Dr. John R. Adolph, Reverend Dr. Jack C. Gause, William C. Akins, Carolyn Bailey, Dr. Robert and Tanuya Worthy, Drs. Abbe Boring, Morcease Beasley, Ruben Olivarez, Stanton Lawrence, Walter Milton, Jr., Sharon Desmoulin-Kherat, and

Queinnise Miller. In addition, I have been blessed and influenced by my interactions with extraordinary individuals, such as Poet Maya Angelou and United States Ambassador to the United Nations Andrew Young. I am eternally grateful for the assistance and support of my family: my wife, Carolyn Jean (Reese) Brown; son, Berlin Lee Brown; daughters, Mary Katherine (Brown) Ruegg and Reesha Johnette (Brown) Edwards; son-in-law, Kyle Ruegg and his parents, Steve and Robin Ruegg; and son-in-law, Desmond Edwards and his parents; granddaughter, Abigail Sage Ruegg; and birth family members, including my mother, Mary Minnie (Bass) Brown, my father, Lee Boyd Brown, Sr., sisters, Joyce Marie and Anita Lynne Brown, and brothers, Lee Boyd Brown, Jr., Willie Arthur and Anthony Wayne Brown, and their spouses.

Introduction and Overview

BIBLICAL REFERENCE ON FAITH

Now faith is the substance of things hoped for, the evidence of things not seen. For by it the elders obtained a good report. Through faith we understand that the worlds were framed by the word of God, so that things which are seen were not made of things which do appear. (Hebrews 11: 1-3)

While growing up as a child I had visions of a world where equality meant equality for all, within and across all aspects of life, especially, in the United States of America. I wondered then, and I continue to question, the reasoning behind people being treated a certain way based upon class -- group classification or sorting according to commonly held beliefs on wealth, characteristics, historical understandings -- and race. I thought often about what role I could play to influence society toward such a reality of equality so that all concerned would enjoy a higher quality of life and happiness. My childhood experience was mostly one of joy and happiness and strength, undergirded by love of family, friends and Christianity. It was also a time of disappointment and regrets for how much we were, and continue to be, affected and driven by considerations of race, class, and social dynamics. The time has come for a major shift in how we treat one another as human beings of equal value and importance. We will all enjoy a higher quality of life when we focus more on the common good and less on considerations of race and class and selfish benefits. The appropriate and progressive way to look at diversity is to celebrate and appreciate it. My belief is that the best and most impactful path to a higher quality of life is through successfully educating all our children -- "all means all!" So far, the plans commonly in place for educating our children fall short in the desired results, and many children miss the opportunity to become educated successfully. I still believe it can happen; I have kept the faith – in things hoped for and the evidence of things not yet seen.

This book presents a set of reflections and ideas for better educating our children. It is also about Emerson Street -- neighborhood and name of the street of my home growing up in Austin, Texas -- and it is about race, class, quality of life, and faith. Part of any effective plan for educating children is fueled and buttressed by the level of expectations. High standards and expectations must be the level required for all schools and classrooms, with no exceptions. Such expectations should be supported by and achieved through high quality teachers, resources, and productive learning environments, where every student has access to opportunities to succeed. In many schools and school districts, the expectations are far too low for some segments of the population, especially in low income and minority communities. It is common for educators and parents to make assumptions that for the students who attend certain schools, especially in the suburbs, the expectations and standards and level of success should be high while in other schools, like those in inner city neighborhoods, just the opposite.

The practice of setting different expectations and learning standards, based upon or related to the income level of the neighborhood, zip code, or racial makeup is quite common and often based upon a culture where failure is not only expected; it is wrongly accepted as a reality that is not under our control. For example, in the high school I attended -- Original L. C. Anderson High School, only certain students were permitted to attend the so-called high level or advanced level courses, such as physics and calculus. This practice was not a black-white consideration which is often the case, as there were only black students in the school. Such a practice was reflective of lower expectations and requirements. Students passed by the advanced class level classrooms and admired the equipment for experiments and reports of coursework, but many of the students were not eligible by school rules to participate. Those types of rules remain in existence across the United States, where we block out students from enjoying certain aspects of the curriculum experiences, based upon rules and practices used to segregate or track students into their designated groups or perceived ability levels. Such practices are wrong now and were wrong then. I happen to believe things can change; I have kept the faith -- in things hoped for and the evidence of things not yet seen. Faith matters now and always!

At some point during each school year in our schools, we place all the students at the testing "table" and require them to take the same standardized tests and wonder why some students perform better than others. Think about it. Some children prepare for those tests by learning and practicing in a "luxury automobile" style environment while others prepare by way of a "bicycle" style environment. There is no mystery why gaps exist in the test scores because the gaps in performance are quite predictable, based on the kinds of inequitable learning experiences.

I can recall an example of the inequalities of educational opportunities during my experiences as superintendent. One district had rules in place that algebra for high school credit would only be offered in certain middle schools and not in others. The course was the same as the one offered in the high schools. Such privileged middle schools were primarily in one section of the school district, the more affluent area of the community. Very tense conversations occurred in the community about these inequitable conditions, even when some of us just raised the issue for public discussion. Some of the parents from the upper income communities complained that by offering the algebra course in some neighborhoods -- so-called less fortunate -- would place too much stress and strain on those students. Their real concern appeared to be interest in their neighborhood children continuing to enjoy the advanced opportunities for preparation and exposure in comparison with the children in other schools. The parents desired to continue the practice of having their children enjoy the exclusive right to acquire skills to excel above certain peers in later grades. When students completed the high school requirement while still in middle school, they gained an advantage for access to taking higher order coursework prior to graduation from high school. However, as the result of community pressure and engagement, the common good prevailed for leveling the "playing field" for students in all middle schools to become exposed to the same level of opportunities in advanced learning and preparation. The rules were changed to ensure equal opportunities for such coursework for all middle school students. This example is, unfortunately, the norm in schools and school districts across the United States. Such practices serve to limit the growth and development of many of our children, while increasing the learning potential of the other students who have access to the "top" or higher-level curriculum.

The following sections of the book include a description of life, from growing up in Austin, Texas, to the present, ending with suggestions about how to move schools toward a better system of academic success for all children and, thereby, improving the chances for the common good and higher quality of life for all. Also, included is a summary of the Winners Always Practice Program, which is a set of tips on winning strategies for sports games and for life. I still believe things can happen for the better; I have kept the faith – in things hoped for and the evidence of things not yet seen.

The consideration of one's color of skin is pervasive within and across all aspects of social dynamics, sometimes deliberate and at other times through unintentional -- but real -- attitudes that are ingrained. It is instructive to seek out persons of color and ask about their impressions of employment or political candidates of color who have been selected for a high level administrative or public positions, especially when they present records of excellent qualifications and high-level preparations. It would not be uncommon to find joy, excitement, and surprise, as so often such high-level jobs do not go to people of color. Then follow with the question of the impressions of when it appears that a person of color is not selected or demoted, based upon what appears to be race and class considerations, over qualifications -- disappointing, but not surprising. Ask the same questions of a person not of color. Often, the answers will be the same, regretful reality but not surprising. There are not enough people in leadership positions who are passionate on this issue and willing to manage or direct the planning and actions, as required for progress, for selection procedures to become fair and equitable. A person should not be selected or rejected for a position or role in life because of race.

The time will be welcomed when all can get beyond any perceptions, let alone realities, that employment or political selections and reactions are based upon or affected by color versus qualifications. Clearly, qualifications, not color, should be the standard every time, noting, it is not always about race. Sometimes, the program or process is fair and reasonable, and we do ourselves no favors to make assumptions or react negatively when facts and data are available and have been clearly applied in making decisions for personnel selections. In human relations endeavors, the process should always be fair, equitable, and designed to employ the most qualified person as basic tenets, or count on facing confusion and lack of confidence in the system and in the persons selected. I have unfortunately encountered situations in job searches where I was not selected and left to ponder whether the process was fair and whether race or class was a determining factor in the decision. I tried in each case to remember my faith in terms of things hoped for, the evidence of things not seen, and convinced myself that what is meant for me will happen.

Consider leisure or fun activities and organizations, such as sports or athletics, at all levels, from grade school to professional career level. The racial makeup of the owners, coaches, quarterbacks in football (although, some progress has been made in recent years), presidents, vice-presidents, chief executive officers of organizations, and similar positions reflects little diversity. That reality matters in deciding whether the "playing field" is fair and equitable for opportunities to excel in employment and leadership. It matters in terms of how this aspect is viewed and perceived by all concerned, especially children as they dream about opportunities and success in career options.

The images portrayed by media and public reports of people of authority and wealth are routinely not people of color, partly because so few people of color hold such positions. Should there be a more diverse makeup of the leadership of organizations within and across race and gender? Yes, diversity matters; equal and equitable access to opportunities matters. Appearance matters. The images impact our thinking of what a successful individual and person of power and authority looks like. Beyond what it looks like, there is an issue of economic prosperity and wealth. All people want to enjoy such status of a good job and economic comfort, but many are held back in finding such a path to such a reality due, at least partly, to issues of race and class.

When a minority or female candidate is selected for a key leadership position, it is often welcomed by many and questioned by others -- as related to race, class, or gender. Many applauded the selection of the first person of color to serve as President of the United States of America, Barack H. Obama. Since that time, questions proven to be invalid and unfair have abounded about the selection and about his job performance, often in unflattering terms. Such questions have gone beyond and have occurred more frequently than that which was experienced by his predecessors or successor – again, emphasizing the term invalid. How much of it can be attributed to his color? No way to really pinpoint it. Race politics have long dominated the views and conduct of many people in America and other countries. Again, consider the treatment by so many, even among those of color, in questioning President Obama's credentials, his birthplace and his decisions while in office, including comments made by his successor. Fair and justified? At least some of it appears to be based on race. In fact, President Obama is of mixed races, born of a White mother and African father. His academic preparation and intellect rival any president of the United States and chief executive officer of any other organization. However, even with such high credentials as he has attained, his color seems to affect the views of many. Unfortunately, it appears that this negativity exists only because his selection placed someone in the office who simply looks different from all other presidents of the United States before him.

The fact that the public would select as president of the United States a successor whose preparation and qualifications paint such a different picture is most revealing of the attitudes and what some people are willing to accept about a person who is not of color. If one were to compare and contrast the preparation and leadership style of President Obama and his successor, the differences would be wide on issues such as the following: (a) concern about race relations, celebration of diversity and welcoming of immigrants into this country; (b) approach taken in strengthening integration of groups in the country and the narrowing of separation of the races; (c) interactions with foreign leaders; and (d) level of priority in focusing on the common good. The idea that such comparisons have been commonly made is reason for pause and reflection, especially given the remarkable results under President Obama's leadership and given the results under the leadership of his successor. Again, there is good reason to admire President Obama as a person of poise, grace, and intelligence who shows concern for other people. His successor was the third United States President impeached by the House of Representatives of the United States Congress and, yet, not convicted by the Senate.

The advice I received as a youngster by teachers and family was that as a person of color, I had to be much better prepared to be considered as qualified as a person not of color. That turned out to be good advice. Far too often, I have observed that race and class often override other considerations. Hopefully, this book will provide enlightenment about the experiences that could hold one back but demonstrate how to attain excellence regardless of the circumstances. I believe things can change for the better; I have kept the faith – in things hoped for and the evidence of things not yet seen. Throughout the book I have included references to faith as "food for thought" and also as part of the Winners Always Practice Program to serve as a reminder that most things are not that serious and it is better not to get "stuck" on small matters. "Let it go!" Move on to the next issue. Keep the faith.

Chapter One

Growing Up and Life Experiences on Emerson Street

I was born and reared in Austin, Texas, and lived a large part of my childhood in a house located on Emerson Street, along with my parents, Mary Minnie (Bass) Brown and Lee Boyd Brown, Sr. (both deceased), three brothers, Lee Boyd Brown, Jr., Willie Arthur Brown (deceased), Anthony Wayne Brown, and two sisters, Joyce Marie Brown and Anita Lynne Brown (deceased). In my mother's family there were six children: five daughters, Mary, Jessie, Pearline, Susie Jane, and Emma Lee; and one son, Elijah Thomas Bass, Jr. My father had two brothers, Wilbert and Elmo, and one sister, Mamie Ray Judson. My grandparents are all deceased: Lindsey Brown and Bessie Davis of Creedmoor, Texas, and Susie and Elijah Thomas Bass of Bryan, Texas. My maternal great grandparents were Melinda Cunningham and Bob Moore. The names of my paternal great grandparents were not available at the time of publication.

The times are quite different now compared with when my mother was born in Bryan, Texas. For example, my mother fondly spoke about the circumstances of her birth. Hospital? No. Her birth in the year 1920 was at her home with the assistance of a mid-wife, a common practice at that time, as hospitals either blocked, totally, or gave limited access to hospital care for people of color. Her home also did not have a regular bathroom equipped with a toilet -- outhouse only -- for bathroom necessities. However, the environment was a positive model of family love and caring for one another, Christian values, and stability. The surroundings were humble with limitations of available resources. My mother's memory was excellent, up to the day and time of her dying in November 2019. She made extraordinary efforts to meet and know any and everybody she could. Part of her routine conversation with others was about how proud she was of her children. My mother, as an adult, was a housewife working sporadically, at times, in sewing and domestic jobs to help make ends meet.

My father was from humble surroundings and circumstances and limited resources, but I learned in conducting research for this book that his birth family had truly little money and lived in a shack of a house. He seldom talked about his birth family or the place where he was born and reared. He was a hard worker and perfectionist at every task he took on -- no excuses mentality. He loved reading and following up with building projects he pulled from his favorite magazine, Popular Mechanics. He held common laborer jobs as an adult, including working at a shipyard munitions plant in California during World War II, in a lumber company in Austin, Texas, and at The University of Texas in housekeeping. Father worked 17 years with great success and loyalty at the lumber company before facing dismissal, for no cause stated or shared, except that the company management believed it had the power to make the decision and was moving in a different direction. At that time, it was more difficult to make ends meet, but through pride, determination, and prayer he landed another job in a few weeks as a custodian at The University of Texas. He was so determined and dedicated that he walked to and from work each day. My father worked hard every day and provided a model for the children in the family of the importance of "a hard day's work for a day's pay".

Mother and Father demonstrated love, respect, and support for each other and for my sisters, brothers, and me every day, and we demonstrated the same toward them and each other and currently with our own children. My parents also consistently demonstrated that same love and concern in reaching out to help other people. Their model of service mentality to help others was an extremely impressive daily display of operating on a values-based foundation rather than focusing on money and other tangible considerations. My mother came to Austin at 18 years of age in 1938 from her home in Bryan, Texas, to attend Tillotson College. She met our dad in church, and they married a couple of years later, in 1940. They went to the courthouse to for the ceremony, deciding to marry on their own prior to informing their parents. My mother borrowed a dress from one of her sisters to wear for the wedding. The judge initially refused to perform the wedding ceremony but acquiesced later the same day to officiate the event. She was 99 years old at the time of her passing, again - born in 1920, and my dad was 71 years old when he passed away, born in 1912, during the time of Jim Crow laws full of segregationist policies and practices.

There were basic values and rules of life practiced and appreciated by my birth family, including Christianity, honesty, hard work ethics, respect for self and others, and the desire to achieve excellence as a way of life. There was an obvious divine connection for the union of my father and mother, as they met in St. Peter's United Methodist Church in Austin, where both were actively involved as church leaders. Both were excellent students in grade school. My mother attended school for a few years at Tillotson College in Austin. My father was an avid reader and deep thinker, and he loved science, gardening, and carpentry.

My family from birth to the present has demonstrated dignity, poise and high standards and values always, including extraordinary self-discipline among my parents and siblings. My brothers, sisters, and I always demonstrated respect and cooperation with our parents; no serious discipline issues ever existed. My parents showed respect for themselves and others at home and elsewhere -- excellent role models always. Their major priorities were spending quality time with and taking care of my brothers, my sisters, and me. They fully understood the value of our earning a good education, and they devoted time and attention to encourage us to attend school every day and to do our best in our schoolwork. My parents also made a point of constantly sharing with us the value and importance of reaching out to help other people.

My birth family was economically challenged in terms of money and resources but spiritually and morally strong through our faith and common bonds of support for one another. The neighborhood included other families of similar backgrounds and circumstances, and it was common for adults to support and correct the neighborhood children. The children complied with such requests and directions. The Emerson Street neighborhood was a friendly one, where everyone for blocks in either direction was acquainted and supportive.

My wife, Carolyn, and I are fortunate to continue to enjoy our marriage of many years and our three wonderful, successful children, one son and two daughters. Each is a high school and college graduate and fortunate to have enjoyed gainful employment soon after their college experiences. Their names are as follows: son, Berlin Lee Brown; and daughters, Mary Katherine (Brown) Ruegg and Reesha Johnette (Brown) Edwards, all three sharing grandparents' or parents' names. Our son was named for Carolyn's father's first name, and his middle name came from my father's first name. Mary's name came from my mother's first name, and her middle name came from Carolyn's mother's first name. The name Reesha was created from Carolyn's maiden name, Reese, and her middle name came from my first name, Johnny. Our oldest daughter, Mary, is married to Kyle Ruegg, and our youngest daughter, Reesha, is married to Desmond Edwards. Our only granddaughter was born June 22, 2019, one day following my birthday, June 21. Again, in a case of divine intervention, Carolyn and I first met at The University of Texas, as she was there as a graduate student, and I was attending Texas State University as a graduate student. Both of us were taking advantage of the opportunity to study on the University of Texas campus.

The Emerson Street life's story is one that I mostly enjoyed and would re-live in full if given the opportunity. Those who enjoyed similar environments and experiences in growing up will understand without much explanation; although, the reminders will be hopefully refreshing. For all others, this book will reveal some truths and viewpoints that may not have otherwise been realized. In the last sections of the book, I share ideas from the Winners Always Practice Program on tips for success and winning in sports and life. I also share carefully crafted suggestions about how to make improvements in education and business leadership.

4

Admittedly, it took many years of living before the story of the location of my real first home would be revealed to me, beyond what I can remember from my childhood experiences. I had just enjoyed one of my adult birthdays by spending time with family, discussing the writing of this book which included reference to what I remembered to be the original, first home I lived in. A debate ensued among the elder members of the family about how long the family had lived first in a house located on Comal Street, somewhere between a few months to a couple of years. Neither the discussion nor circumstance of the revelation was unusual. Sensitive topics were not always discussed either openly or loudly in the family, especially among youth, unless relevant to the present situation or helpful for needed clarification.

Apparently, what made this story sensitive was that my father and mother were not the owners of the house in which my brothers and sisters and I first lived. I was born in 1948, three years after World War II ended. My oldest brother, Lee Boyd, Jr., was born in 1942; brother, Willie, was born in 1943, both born during the time of war; and Joyce was born in September 1945, a few months after the war ended. The challenges were obviously great for many people, as the nation continued to rebound from the period of The Great Depression and considering the circumstances and impact of war. Occupants of the Comal Street house included my parents, an aunt, cousin, grandparents, and siblings -- a full house. The parents were careful not to engage the children in discussions on matters of which pride may have an effect on the children's self-confidence, worthiness, or strength or which may in some way may distract from the focus on growth, development, or the learning process.

The Brown family has come a long way since our experiences before and after we moved to the house located on Emerson Street. We were fortunate to always enjoy nice houses to live in, Comal Street, Emerson Street and more recently, Basford Road. When we lived on Comal Street, we had three bedrooms, a den, a courtyard, and a fishpond, with fish in it, where neighbors and friends actually fished. The pond was encircled by bricks, giving it a very pleasing appearance. This structure was put in place in the 1940s, and my father was responsible for building most of it. No others in the neighborhood had a pond like ours. The Comal Street house was on a corner lot and had nice hedges bordering the yard.

At some point during my early childhood years, in the 1950s, the family moved into what became the first home owned by my mother and my father -- yes -- located at 1908 Emerson Street, a street adjacent to Comal Street. Literally, the house located on Emerson Street was a few steps away from the house on Comal Street, just past two houses away. Our dad had a vision of what the house could become on Emerson Street and he, initially, purchased the lot on which the house would eventually sit. The house structure -- formerly duplex structure -- was transported from downtown Austin in two parts, that is, one part of the house was transported, followed by the other half a few weeks later. Dad, literally, merged the house sections of the duplex together, working late into the nights until the house was ready for occupancy. He worked at night because he was, at the time, working at his regular job at the lumber company during the day. The process took over a year for completion. The house had ten-foot ceilings and multiple steps to climb from ground floor to the top of the porch. The house had a pigeon coop, work shed, flowers and shrubbery all over the yard, and other nice features. A huge garage and covered patio were added later, all constructed by my father. My two sisters enjoyed sleeping in one bedroom, and my oldest brother and I shared a bedroom on the other side of the house. After my brother, Lee Boyd, left for the military, the room was shared with my younger brother. Before I moved into the room with my oldest brother, Lee Boyd, Jr., I had been sleeping in the same room as my parents. My second oldest brother, Willie, had a bedroom in one corner of the house which was, literally, built by the hands of our dad, at about the same time he built the dining room. The bedroom had initially been built for the occupancy of my grandfather, but in the end my brother, Willie, used that room instead.

We had an attractive dining room and smaller breakfast room area and kitchen. No hot water heater was installed, and we boiled water for bathing and cooking. The house we lived in on Comal Street was owned by my grandmother, Bessie Davis (we called her Mamma Bessie) who died in 1952, prior to our moving to the Emerson Street location. She also owned the house located behind the one we lived in on Comal

Street. After my grandmother's dying, conflict and confusion surfaced concerning ownership and who would make decisions about the two houses; she did not leave a will. My cousin, Gloria, who had been living in our house got married to Tim Pierce and left town to teach. She claimed ownership of the two houses, followed by putting the house we were living in up for lease. The other house in the scenario was already being rented out to non-family members. Although the house on Emerson Street was not totally ready for occupancy, we moved from the house on Comal Street to the house on Emerson Street. Our dad and Gloria and her husband did not communicate for several years following the debate about our moving out of the house we were forced to leave. Gloria's mother, my aunt, Mamie Ray Judson, was my father's sister, but Gloria lived in the house on Comal with her grandparents, my father's parents, instead of with her parents before leaving town to teach. It appears that Gloria never knew her father; her recollection of her upbringing was that of a child being born and left with a grandmother for rearing.

My birth family still resides in Austin not far from the Emerson Street location. The reason we moved from the house on Emerson Street in 1969 was due to a government urban renewal program, where we were required to move in favor of what would later become a local university athletic baseball field, which is the current site of baseball games for The University of Texas. We lived in the Emerson Street house for about 16 years before being forced by the government to move. We kept the faith – in things hoped for and the evidence of things not yet seen. We believed throughout the transition in being forced to move from one place to another that things would work out fine—and it turned out that we were correct.

Our family enjoyed a lot of love each day living in Austin in both of our houses on Emerson and Comal Streets. We were challenged economically but never went hungry. Daily meal menus often included several variations of beans, that is, beans and rice, beans and rice with ground beef, sausage or chicken. The most routine main courses served included fried chicken, meatloaf, spaghetti, hot dogs, sausage, and, almost always, vegetables and sometimes fruit. Did we enjoy multiple television sets during my early growth years? No, we owned only one set, a black and white television, and we owned a radio. Currently, perhaps, in a form of silent protest, or living the dream, my family members living in Austin and I now enjoy possession of multiple television sets -- color, of course -- in our places of residence.

While we applauded and enjoyed nice features in the house, there was no air conditioner in place for comfort during the summer in the house on Emerson Street. During the winter, heat was available in only designated sections of the house. Did we have a hot water heater available for bathing? No. We boiled water on the kitchen stove and transported it to the bathroom for bathing. We were thankful for and still appreciate many years later the use of products such as Ivory soap, which was less expensive than other brands, and it worked well with sensitive skin, beyond babies' needs. At times lye soap came in handy and would be used to clean just about anything -- body and clothes as well. Did we enjoy a clothes dryer in the house? No. We placed wet clothes on the wire line outside, which was strung across tree limbs. Sometimes the washing machine worked, and at other times we used a bucket into which we would place the clothes for washing. How about possession, availability and use of an automobile, routinely, to travel to and from school and other places? No. Dad drove a truck to and from work when it worked, and we owned a station wagon which seldom worked. We walked to and from school each day from elementary through high school. The elementary school, Campbell, was located only a few blocks away from the Emerson Street house, and the junior high school was not much farther – but in a different direction. The high school was about five miles away. But my sisters and brothers and I attended school every day and never complained about the inconvenience of traveling by foot to and from school and to other places we had to go, rain or shine, during cold or hot weather conditions.

Medical care was always strong and available in growing up while living on Emerson Street. We enjoyed a positive relationship with our family doctor, Dr. Bud Dryden, who was my doctor from birth through high school. He was friendly and used direct language in his approach to providing medical care for his patients. His office was located across the street from the local hospital, Brackenridge Hospital - the original building no longer in operation and replaced by a newer facility. I can recall times when customers approached Dr. Dryden in the hallway with questions about their health, and he always answered, "I don't doctor in the hallway", thereby, assuring the privacy of the customers and avoiding delays in following the established daily schedule.

Success in becoming educated was stressed throughout my childhood and beyond -- reminded even during adulthood of its importance. Not surprisingly, therefore, the Brown and Reese (wife, Carolyn's family) families enjoy a nice story of success in the form of family members who completed high school and have attended and earned college degrees. My mother attended two years of college at Tillotson College in Austin. My oldest brother, Lee Boyd Brown, Jr. attended college at Texas Christian University, the University of Kentucky, and St. Edwards University, and he was recruited for a track scholarship by Michigan State University. My youngest sister, Anita, attended college at Southwest Texas State University and did very well, interrupted only by her death due to illness. My second oldest brother, Willie, attended and graduated from Huston-Tillotson College and was a college athlete -- basketball. He completed his master's degree at Prairie View A & M University. He was serving as a school principal in San Bernardino, California, at the time of his death. My oldest sister, Joyce, attended and graduated from Huston-Tillotson College (now named University), no longer separated by gender, which was the arrangement when my mother was in college. Huston was for the men, and Tillotson was the campus for women. Joyce completed the master's degree at Prairie View A & M University. My youngest brother, Anthony, attended and graduated from The University of Texas at Austin with his bachelor's degree.

On Carolyn's side of the family, she, her sister Joan and three brothers, Billy, Michael, and Frederick attended college, each of them earning an associate degree from Paris Junior College. Carolyn, her sister, Joan, Frederick, and Billy earned bachelor's degrees. Carolyn and her sister earned master's degrees.

Carolyn and I are proud of our children, as all have attended and earned college degrees. Berlin graduated from The University of Alabama at Tuscaloosa with a degree in electrical engineering. Mary graduated from Texas State University with a degree in computer graphics. Reesha graduated from The University of West Georgia with a degree in communications for the bachelor's degree and from The University of Houston with a Master of Arts in Communications degree. My nephews and nieces tout an impressive record of college attendance as well. Lee Boyd, Jr.'s son, Michael, is a college graduate as is his wife, Deidre; Lee Boyd III attended college. At the date of publication two of Lee Boyd, Jr.'s grandchildren are attending college: Donovan is a student at Drake University, and Olivia is a student at Rhodes College. Anthony's children, Mychal, Haley, Blake, and Taylor are all college graduates. Regarding my brother, Willie, his younger daughter, Carol, graduated with a bachelor's degree, and Carla, his older daughter, graduated with her bachelor's, master's degrees, and a doctorate. The educational achievements continue with the younger generations of the Brown and Reese families, some of whom remain in high school.

Chapter Two

Family Joy, Excitement
and Proud Moments

There have been moments of joy and excitement and of stress and disappointment -- where race or color was a factor or force behind adult behavior. I prefer to start with sharing the joyful. I was fortunate to grow up in an environment where family and friends were supportive and encouraging of my being able to participate in special activities and events as a teenager at the city coliseum and Municipal Auditorium in Austin, such as performances by entertainers like James Brown and boxing matches on live stream by Muhammad Ali. I had barely enough money to enter, but somehow it worked out -- priceless exposure to crowds and excellence in performances. I enjoyed my childhood and remember fondly the routine associations with people who demonstrated that they cared for me and my welfare including, but not limited to, family, church members, school employees and classmates, and community. The joy has continued in adulthood due to many of the same reasons and associations.

There are far too many joyful moments to comment on related to family, school and neighborhood activities and events -- some in faith-based settings and others in non-faith-based settings. I consider myself fortunate that in all cases my experiences with birth family and family through matrimony, friends, church, community, and teachers have been, remarkably positive, and memorable. In one thoughtful demonstration of showing love and concern by my father, he passed on to me his last $50.00 which he had been saving for dental work as I left home for college. The college only provided the student athletes $7.00 per month to be used for laundry and incidental expenses. The memories of such sacrifices by my mother and father have remained with me. When our children are in need, if it is something Carolyn and I may provide, we do so with love and joy in our hearts. The same was done for both of us by our families. I have kept the faith – in things hoped for and the evidence of things not yet seen.

The marriage to my wife of many years, Carolyn, has been most inspirational and a joyful experience. The Reese family welcomed me with open arms and has always made efforts to make me feel like a true member of the family. The Browns have made similar efforts in welcoming Carolyn into our family.

The birth of each one of our three wonderful children was a source of pure joy, pride, and excitement. Each of them has enjoyed success in elementary and secondary school and beyond, including the joy of graduation from college and success as adults. The marriages of our oldest daughter, Mary, to Kyle Ruegg and youngest daughter, Reesha, to Desmond McGee Edwards were memorable occasions and joyful for me and Carolyn and the entire family. There was extraordinary excitement and joy with the birth and excellent health of our first granddaughter, Abigail Sage Ruegg, on June 22, 2019. It has been a true pleasure and delight to observe her in growing up -- a week, then before we knew it, a month, then two and six months, and a year and beyond. We are counting the days, now enjoying seeing her walking and talking and inching steadily toward that of becoming a woman of great intelligence and success. She is kind, smart and strong.

Carolyn and I are fortunate to have a son, daughters, and sons-in-law who are strong in use of technology, as they encourage and give tips routinely on the latest gadgets and their use and keep us anchored and up to date, in particular, associated with communications and music devices. Carolyn and I were wise to give gifts relating to technology to our son and daughters during their childhood years -- including computers. We did not strongly promote the idea of Santa Claus, but, instead, we asked them what they wanted for Christmas. They did not disappoint in listing the things they asked for, in terms of usefulness and reasonable cost per gift. Electronics were always high on their lists.

The joy of watching our son and two daughters participating in extracurricular activities in high school produced a lifetime of positive memories. Berlin was on the football team at Saint Ignatius High School in Cleveland, Ohio, whose team won the state and national championships during his freshman year on the team (experienced a serious arm injury during one of their tough tackling drills). He also played on the football team at Bowie High School in Austin, Texas and on a baseball team as a young teenager. Berlin was also a member of the band at St. Ignatius High School. I can vividly recall his marching in the band in downtown Cleveland during a parade and his playing in the band during the graduation ceremony, which featured the senior class and their parents. Each graduate announced where he (males only school) would attend college and each was greeted on stage by his parents upon receiving the diploma -- outstanding ceremony. Our oldest daughter, Mary, played in the bands at Bowie High School in Austin and Ramsay High School in Birmingham, Alabama, and tennis team at Ramsay. I can still gladly recall Mary's precision and skills in marching with the band at Bowie High School and how well the band performed at Ramsay High School. Mary was also part of a praise dancing squad in college and played on the basketball team while in middle school. Reesha played on the basketball team and was in the band while attending Lakeside High School, and she played in the band at Ramsay High School in Birmingham. I can recall several of her performances while playing in the band at both schools. Reesha experienced the unfortunate challenge and reality of having to pass the high school graduation examination for two states, Alabama and Georgia. Of course, she did well in both states, yet unreasonable stress was imposed. Again, joyful, and memorable experiences for sure for each of our three children.

Our son and daughters were good students in school and well-disciplined from birth through grade school and college. They have continued in adulthood to demonstrate the best in self-discipline and awareness of what is and is not important. Among other areas of pride and jubilation in watching them grow and prosper, I am pleased about their proven attitudes and appreciation of other people -- of all races, creeds, and backgrounds. The modeling my wife and I and family demonstrated must have paid off and, at least, did not confuse them. They consistently show an interest in getting along with and respecting people of different races. It was pleasing, therefore, to experience it when our youngest daughter attended the high school prom at Lakeside High School with young ladies of differing backgrounds and races. Carolyn and I were more than happy to sponsor the limousine for their travel. Our oldest daughter's baby shower for our granddaughter, Abigail, was also a picture-perfect mosaic of diversity in spanning the room of participants. And, our son is friends with and spends time with a diverse group of employees from his company. The joy was overwhelming of seeing our son and daughters' experiences of dressing up for and attending their high school proms.

You cannot put a price high enough to match or compare with the value of the numerous unforgettable opportunities for fun and bonding that Carolyn, our son and daughters and I had in enjoying picnics at various parks, albeit, some of the time during these outings, the temperature was a bit chilly. Yet, today we regret not going more often. The hill country in Metro-Austin, with its rolling hills and lakes is beautiful and exhilarating, allowing a memorable connection with nature. We also enjoyed time together in taking family vacations to places such as the following: Disneyland in California and Disneyworld and other entertainment events in the state of Florida; the Grand Canyon and Las Vegas in the state of Nevada; traveling to places like, Canada, New York, Connecticut, Arkansas, New Jersey, and the Smoky Mountains of Tennessee; Philadelphia, Pennsylvania; Rhode Island; New Hampshire; South Carolina; North Carolina; Virginia; New Mexico; Arizona; and Massachusetts; Nassau, Bahamas; and Washington, D. C. We took a trip that included our son, daughter, and their husbands during the same time as one of my birthday celebrations (nice coincidence). The trip included a visit to the Smithsonian Museum – National African American Museum of History and Culture. We have also enjoyed living in four states: Texas, Ohio, Alabama, and Georgia.

As with my own children, the students in school districts where I have worked have been a source of pride and fulfillment. I have genuinely enjoyed watching those children grow up and succeed in elementary and secondary school and college and enjoying success in their chosen careers. Among other exhilarating moments, I have marveled at hearing reports of youth in securing lucrative job opportunities, especially when those jobs entailed contracts for salaries of $100,000 to $1,000,000 and more. I am equally as proud of hearing of the other stories of upward mobility of our youth when they have found gainful employment at any level, as it is not so much about the money as it is quality of life, joy and happiness. The youth I have worked with and supervised have come primarily from humble, low-income situations, so all of these moments of joy have been reflections of what can happen when you work hard, study your school lessons and make wise life choices.

When I graduated from high school, it was a nice celebration and "bridge" from life on Emerson Street toward life in college and beyond. The high school was segregated by race, having only African American students, and I was the first athlete of color at the college I attended. The public grade school experience was incredibly positive from elementary through high school, with graduation from the Original L.C. Anderson High School being a special highlight of joy, as was participation on the high school basketball team and selection as team captain. I was ecstatic upon being selected to the high school basketball team and honored to wear the team uniform, including the Converse All Star Tennis Shoes -- which continue to be a popular shoe brand among youth. I was also honored to be selected as an athlete for the high school All-District Team and Prairie View Interscholastic League All-Star Game in Houston as a senior student. In addition, I was pleased to be named by our high school coach as the Player of the Year as a senior in 1966, receiving the Coach L. M. Britton Player of the Year Basketball Award. The "Class of 1966" of the Original L. C. Anderson High School was a special group. The parents, faculty and staff did an excellent job in encouraging the members in the Class of 1966 to treat each other with respect, appreciation, and dignity, and we gladly accepted such instruction and guidance. We did not separate by "class" or neighborhood origins or by who participated on which team or club or otherwise. We communicated within and across various units as students and as adults. Even as this book is written the "Class of 1966" communicates monthly through benefit of a prayer conference call. During the call we share how classmates are doing, and we share bible verses and words of encouragement. I was fortunate to enjoy excellent teachers and principals throughout my elementary and secondary school experiences. Each faculty and staff member treated other students and me with dignity and respect and demonstrated concern for our learning success and growth and development.

It was an honor to be recruited by The University of Texas at Austin to play basketball right in the middle of a transitional period for the integration of colleges and universities in many places across the nation; although, I did not accept the offer. I was just as pleased about the recruitment by both Paul Quinn College in Waco and Bishop College in Dallas, Texas, and other schools -- noting that Paul Quinn College re-located several years later to the site of Bishop College in Dallas. I decided to attend Texas State University (then named Southwest Texas State University), the recruitment and enrollment of which were a special honor, as I would become the first African American athlete at the school. The coaches and athletic director were cordial and supportive throughout the recruitment process and my time in college. The teammates and I got along well, and we had great times in conversations about our families, growing up during childhood and challenges and disappointments. We especially enjoyed the special meals we were privileged to be part of, such as those provided during holidays when the school cafeterias were closed. The school was away from home but not very far away and not too difficult for visitations by me to home and by family to the school. The basketball coach at The University of Texas who sought to recruit me to play for the school was still the coach upon my graduation from the university I attended, and I was honored later to become the high school basketball coach of his son in Austin.

Was I a talented basketball player? Humbly, the answer is yes. I could play then, and I am still a good shooter, albeit at a much slower pace, of course. My favorite shot in high school and college was from either corner, near the baseline. I was also a good free throw shooter then and have retained those skills through today. This is relevant partly because of the growth and development in childhood in modest surroundings, that is, basket in my backyard and opportunities to practice at my local elementary school. There the baskets were not regulation height, and the playing surface was concrete. I thought as a child and continued as an adult to always think like a champion—if you can believe it, you can achieve it mentally and physically!

Graduation from college was certainly refreshing and a true joy in each instance: undergraduate and master's degrees and post-graduate schooling at Texas State University and doctorate from The University of Texas at Austin, as well as post-graduate work at Lamar University. Most exhilarating, of course, was the achievement of earning the terminal degree, Doctor of Philosophy, from The University of Texas at Austin. The University is in the same neighborhood where Emerson and Comal Streets were located, and the university baseball field sits on the site where those streets existed during my childhood.

I earned the highest academic recognition, straight "A's" in graduate studies at The University of Texas and Lamar University and only one "B" and otherwise straight "A's" for all other graduate level grades at Texas State University, during my Master of Education degree work and post-graduate studies. The dissertation topic at the University of Texas at Austin was <u>Leader Behavior and School Effectiveness</u>. I conducted research at The University of Texas about what urban city school leaders do to make a difference in leadership in instruction and home-school relations, with the cities of focus in the research sample for the dissertation including the school districts in these Texas cities: Austin, Dallas, Fort Worth, and San Antonio. I strongly believe that instructional leadership, home-school relations and being fair and equitable in approach to leadership make a major difference. In those schools in which parents are engaged in a meaningful way, the performance of children is higher. Therefore, I am a strong advocate of the idea of engaging parents and in communicating with parents and students as part of assuring that the conditions are in place for student success. Throughout my education career, I have strongly supported a parent, student, and employee friendly environment in schools. Such support includes my being an advocate for campus and school district policies that address parental engagement in support of student learning. The data reflect increases in parental involvement in each school district for which I served as superintendent. It is important to plan for positive home-school relations and connectivity between the home and school. Again, it has been proven that students perform better academically when there is such a connection. It is also clear that when strong instructional leadership is provided by the superintendent and school principals, the teachers are better able and more inspired to teach successfully.

My selection by peers as the basketball Coach of the Year for the 1976-77 school year in Austin, Texas, was a special honor. More importantly, our student athletes were excellent students in high school and later in college. The team for that year won 24 games and lost 6, winning 15 games and losing only 1 in district play. I was as pleased to be named as a coach in my first teaching and coaching job in San Antonio, Texas, teaching middle school life science and physical education and coaching football, basketball, track, tennis, and swimming. During the first year of coaching our 7th grade teams won first place in the city championship in basketball and second place in football. I left the job in San Antonio to return to my home, Austin, as a middle school coach and social studies teacher and later as teacher and head basketball coach at the high school, located a few miles away. What an honor it was to be named as the first head basketball coach for the current L.C. Anderson High School, same name as my original high school, albeit, in another part of the city.

It was nice to win the games on the basketball court and football field. The greater positive impact was in the relationships that were enjoyed among all of us. We laughed together during joyful moments, and we frowned together -- and even cried -- at times of tragedy and despair. Throughout the time of the experiences as teacher and coach and beyond as an administrator, we celebrated diversity and opportunities to learn from one another in sharing our experiences. Such exposure was immeasurable and possible only because we dared to communicate and spend time together in different settings and situations. Among the other highlights that I may share, one example concerned after work hours and during weekends when we teachers and coaches attended events together and enjoyed conversation and music -- yes, all kinds of music, including soul music, rock and even country and western music. I learned how, for example, to do the country western dance two-step routine and still remember it today. And I continue to hum and pat my feet at the sound of all kinds of music, including soul, rock and roll, country, gospel, Cajun, and opera. I proudly have learned how to do all kinds of line dances. Diversity is a good thing, for sure, and it should be celebrated.

I was excited and honored to be named as education leader in several situations, including the following:

- Assistant principal at Crockett High School in Austin.
- Principal of O. Henry Middle School in Austin -- first African American in the role as principal of the school.
- Associate coordinator of student affairs and later director of student affairs in Austin
- Deputy superintendent in Cleveland, Ohio and executive deputy superintendent in Houston, Texas.
- Superintendent in Wilmer-Hutchins, Texas upon selection by the local school board and state of Texas as part of a state takeover program -- the school district was later closed several years following my departure and merged with the school district in Dallas, Texas.
- Superintendent in Birmingham, Alabama; superintendent in DeKalb County, Georgia, being named as the first African American to hold the position.
- Superintendent in Port Arthur, Texas, upon recruitment by the school board, in coordination with the State of Texas as part of another state takeover program.

The selection in Port Arthur was a joyous occasion, and memorable upon being contacted by the search consultant and informed that the school board wanted to meet with me for an interview. Things got interesting as Carolyn and I sat in a room adjacent to the school board meeting room while they deliberated on whether to approve my selection as the superintendent. We considered leaving prior to the vote and going back home considering some of the comments we had heard.

Once the selection was approved, we were happy about it, although displeased about hearing some of the comments by one school board member who made disparaging remarks, such as she wanted more proof that as superintendent I would truly care about children in Port Arthur and make a positive difference. We decided to remain through the vote, which was in my favor; the school board affirmed the selection. I took the job and remained in the position for seven years. Carolyn joined the staff one year later and remained for twelve years as the English-Language Arts curriculum supervisor, up to the point of her retirement.

I am honored about and proud of the opportunities to meet several United States presidents and being in the company of other presidents, and governors, local city, state, and national elected and other public officials. Among such encounters: meeting several times with Presidents George Herbert Walker Bush, and son, George W. Bush, while working in Houston, Texas, and meeting with President George W. Bush in the White House in Washington, D. C. I was invited to the White House among a few other educators, to discuss the pending approval by Congress of the "No Child Left Behind" legislation in 2001. President George W. Bush held such a meeting to be sure of public exposure to the legislation. By inviting the group to the White House, he reasoned that the media would follow us and report on the meeting; he was correct. I was also invited to other meetings at the White House regarding education reform. The United States Secretary of Education, Dr. Rod Paige, who formerly served as superintendent in Houston made it possible for such exposure and opportunities to meet with President George H. W. Bush and Mrs. Barbara Bush in Houston and with President George W. Bush (and wife, Laura), both as Governor of Texas and as President of The United States. I was most honored to enjoy a tour of the Oval Office in the White House, led by President George W. Bush. I also enjoyed meeting President Barack Obama during a program in Beaumont, Texas. Additionally, I have been involved in programs where other United States presidents were in attendance, including Presidents Lyndon B. Johnson and Bill Clinton, and I was delighted to meet Vice-President Al Gore during the time of the Clinton Administration. Finally, I was invited to the White House for a discussion of the national strategy for supporting reading instruction. Unfortunately, this meeting did not occur, as it was scheduled during the same week as the awful September 11, 2001, attack on our government. Obviously, the meeting was cancelled considering the circumstances.

What a great pleasure and honor it was to appear on a nationally televised town hall meeting about reading instruction in California with the United States Secretary of Education, Richard Riley. Prior to the start of the television program, Secretary Riley hosted a preparation dinner in an invitation only gathering to practice who would play what part in the television program. I also was honored and proud to attend a meeting in the office of former Secretary of Education, Dr. Rod Paige. I was impressed with the office setting and luncheon, which was prepared by the office chef and staff.

Other experiences have been tremendous to enjoy and have had a profound impact in my professional and personal growth and development. Those include the meetings and learning from famous and nationally recognized politicians and community leaders. For example, it was a pleasure to participate in programs and enjoy the company of the wife of civil rights Leader, Dr. Martin Luther King, Jr., Coretta Scott King with his children and other relatives. These were opportunities which will never be forgotten or taken for granted. Mrs. King and I participated in several programs together, and I marveled at her grace and dignified manner and her tendency to be humble and graceful in communications with her. She shared valuable advice about how best to communicate with the media, and I was shocked and proud about her knowledge of my work in education and how much she had read about me prior to our first meeting.

I am also proud to have had opportunities to know and be in meetings and programs with other civil rights leaders, such as the Reverend Dr. Joseph E. Lowery -- founder of the Georgia Coalition for the Peoples' Agenda committee. I served as one of the leaders for the parent educator outreach program for that organization. Additionally, I was proud to attend meetings with civil rights leaders, such as the following: Reverend Jesse Jackson; Reverend Al Sharpton; Mr. Shelley Stewart; Reverend Fred Shuttlesworth; Ambassador Andrew Young; Reverend C. T. Vivian; Congressman John Lewis; Reverend Abraham Woods, Jr.; Reverend James Orange; and Reverend John Porter.

I was fortunate to enjoy participating in meetings and programs with: Former Honorable State Representative and Chairman of the Georgia Black Legislative Delegation, Stan Watson, who later become DeKalb County, Georgia Commissioner; Former Georgia State Supreme Court Chief Justice, Leah Ward Sears; United States Supreme Court Justice, Clarence Thomas, who conducted the swearing in ceremony of Justice Sears in Georgia. I have also been honored to meet other television and nationally recognized personalities, such as Judges Glenda Hatchett and Greg Mathis; national and local National Association for the Advancement of Colored People (NAACP) leaders; Rainbow Coalition representatives; Southern Christian Leadership Conference members and others. One noticeably clear and observable characteristic of those community leaders I spent time with the most, while living in Alabama and Georgia was their propensity to be friendly, humble, and show concern for others. They consistently spoke provocatively and eloquently about promoting justice and equality for all. I am also proud of the work of other organizations with which I have been associated that devote resources and time to improve the quality of life through programs, research and conversations for educating children, targeting our youth of color: 100 Black Men of America (including the Greater Beaumont Chapter of which I am a member and officer); National Alliance of Black School Educators and Texas Alliance of Black School Educators, of which I am a member of both organizations.

While serving as superintendent of schools in Alabama and Georgia, I enjoyed many pleasures of growth in better understanding of and appreciation for the struggles and impact of issues regarding race. I had learned much during my childhood years in Austin, Texas, the university environment and early professional career experiences, but the work and living experiences gained while in Alabama and Georgia were priceless in molding who I have become as a person and an educator. One immeasurable type of exposure was gained through presentations and participation in programs and meetings in Birmingham, Alabama, such as those held at the 16th Street Baptist Church and 6th Avenue Baptist Church. I grew in faith, strength, and knowledge because of my experiences. I have indeed kept the faith – in things hoped for and the evidence of things not yet seen.

I marveled at the opportunity to meet other prominent artists and entertainers: Poet Maya Angelou; Samuel L. Jackson, Phylicia Rashard; Danny Glover; Yolanda Adams; Isaac Hayes; Tom Joyner; Anthony Anderson, and other singers, actors, and actresses. In moments of incredibly special privilege, I enjoyed meeting and being in the company of entertainer, Jamie Foxx, in his home in California on two occasions. His stepfather was my high school classmate, and I enjoyed the pleasure of being invited to attend two genuinely nice class reunions, hosted at Jamie Foxx's home. We enjoyed his hospitality and memories of our high school years of the mid-1960s. In terms of focus on diversity and positive race relationships, Mr. Foxx and my classmate invited a Mexican Mariachi band to perform for our evening banquet for entertainment during one of our reunion gatherings. The program was excellent, and my classmates and I had a great time dancing and singing to the music as the band performed.

The pleasure of being in athletics has spanned many years, offering the occasional opportunity to meet or be in the presence of various professional athletes and coaches: Tiger Woods; Evander Holyfield; Bill Russell; Shaquille O'Neal; Stephen Jackson; Jamaal Charles; Dave Winfield; Kendrick Perkins; Earl Thomas; Danny Gorrer; John Wooden; Digger Phelps; Bobby Bowden; Darryl Royal; Mack Brown; Abe Lemons; Tony Brown; Elandon Roberts and many others. The University of Texas experience in completion of the doctoral degree also offered numerous events for meeting with and being in the presence of well-known authors and educators, for example, Al Shanker and Phillip Schlechty. The American Educational Research Association has also been instrumental in my exposure to successful, well-known educators and writers, initially connecting through The University of Texas at Austin. Among them it has been my pleasure to engage in projects and communications with many recognized experts: Drs. Linda Darling-Hammond; Gloria Ladsen-Billings; Rod Paige; Jeannie Oakes; Anne Henderson; Joyce Epstein; Robert Marzano; Ruby Payne; Fenwick English; John Goodlad; Daniel Pink; Theodore R. Sizer; Stephen R. Covey; Howard Gardner; Jonathan Kozol; Barbara Foorman; and others. It was my real honor and pleasure to be selected to make a presentation at the annual research conference of the American Educational Research Association, held in Chicago in 1991.

It was also a real pleasure and honor to be selected as an inductee for the Original L. C. Anderson High School Hall of Fame in 2012, of which the selection was made based on my accomplishments as an educator in schools in four states: Texas, Ohio, Alabama, and Georgia. I was also so honored to be selected as the keynote speaker for the annual reunion banquet for that same year. The selection by the Prairie View Interscholastic League Coaches Association for the Hall of Fame Program in 2015 represents one of the finest adult honors, recognizing the successful years and accomplishments as a student athlete, during times of school segregation. The mission of this organization is to preserve the past and celebrate the glorious years of the Prairie View Interscholastic League (PVIL), which existed from 1920 to 1970, during years when schools were segregated by race. The schools of the organization fully merged with the University Interscholastic League upon closure of the PVIL. The awards program was made even more special by the presence of my family -- wife, son and two daughters, son-in-law, and his mother and numerous classmates from my Original L. C. Anderson High School graduating class. The joy was more profound as one of my classmates and friend was also inducted based upon his success in football. Shortly thereafter I was selected to participate as a volunteer consultant to the governing board of the organization and subsequently as a member of the governing board.

I was honored January 9, 2020, to be selected by The University of Texas Division of Diversity and Community Engagement to receive the Legacy Achievement Award during a luncheon at the sixth annual Black Student Athlete Summit. The award is presented each year to a person who has demonstrated success in leading by example for supporting the civil and human rights of others and for "blazing the trails" by helping others enjoy a higher quality of life. I was grateful for the acknowledgement of success in educating our youth and in recognition of the volunteer hours I have spent in providing "service above self". A few days later, January 27, I was honored and proud to be selected by the Department of Educational Leadership and Policy for the Cooperative Superintendency Program (CSP). Alumni Lifetime

Leadership Achievement Award. I was thrilled by the reaction of the young members – mainly college athletes - who comprised much of the audience (at the Black Student-Athlete Summit); they were amazed and awed by the fact that I could share memories of real life experiences that reflected some of the struggles endured by African Americans years after slavery and civil rights legislation in our nation. These honors are a few of the instances where I have felt blessed by experiences which have allowed me to become the person that I am today.

───── *Chapter Three* ─────

Dealing with Stress,
Disappointment and Struggles

No doubt the most stressful times were those circumstances regarding loss of life and illness, especially, among family and friends. Our family has lost my father and mother, as well as one sister and one brother, both of whom were relatively young and experiencing life with enthusiasm at the time of their dying. Also, difficult were the losses and illnesses among other family members: grandparents, aunts, uncles, cousins, nieces, in-laws, and friends. I am reminded about the blessings of enjoying them during the time they were alive and well. Some personal health challenges have made things slightly more difficult for me at times and have served as reminders of who really is in charge -- supreme being -- and who is not. The other disappointments being shared relate primarily to instances where race was a major or perceived factor. I have continued, however, to believe that changes and miracles can happen for the better. I have kept the faith – in things hoped for and the evidence of things not yet seen.

As a teenager during the 1960s, my White neighborhood friend and I went to the local snack bar in a pharmacy located on the Austin, Texas, Interstate Highway 35, a few blocks from my home on Emerson Street.

I was turned away from the snack bar due to policies of segregation and directed to take my drink outside to drink it, while my friend could enjoy his drink at the bar. He left with me, instead. The disappointment of such an experience has lingered for many years. The experience was unfortunately routine among people of color in my neighborhood during my childhood. In sharing a memory of a similar situation, I was a student in an Austin elementary school, where each year we attended symphony orchestra programs downtown at a theatre where the White and non-African American students sat downstairs and African American students were required to sit upstairs -- ensuring segregation of the races. Yet, I learned long ago "Let it go!" Move on to the next issue. I believed positive change could happen and it has; I kept the faith – in things hoped for and the evidence of things not yet seen.

I was stopped in Austin by a local, young police officer in an act of racial profiling even as I was a seasoned, mature adult, at a local bank machine near where my relatives live. After completing my bank business and starting to get into my vehicle, the officer stopped me from getting into the car. He asked embarrassing questions about what I was doing there -- had just returned from getting a haircut, with the smell of oil sheen, clearly, permeating the air. I found it important and necessary to contact the barber on the telephone followed by contacting my wife, whereupon each served as a telephone witness about my immediate whereabouts from which I had just departed. I was still required by the officer to show identification, and he contacted the police station prior to my being able to depart. He said later that he was notified about a bank alarm going off, but, nonetheless, he stopped only me for questioning and not the other people nearby who were not of color. I followed up with his supervisor at the police station who explained that the officer was new and probably nervous and trying to please his department officials. He said he would counsel with the officer about how better to handle situations of that nature in the future. I "Let it go!" Then I moved on to the next issue.

While I was fortunate to be awarded a "full" college scholarship at Texas State University, I was initially assigned for the first semester of school to a dormitory -- Harris Hall -- outside the regular athletic dormitory facilities, due to policies and practices of segregation. I was welcomed to attend the school, but I was not welcomed to live in the dormitory designated for scholarship athletes. At the beginning of the second semester, I was transferred to live in the athletes' dormitory with the other athletes, three to a room. Psychologically, I managed during the first semester experience to believe the glass was at least "full" and even overflowing with the good, certainly much more than "half full", as I was segregated from the other athletes. However, in Harris Hall I had more living space and in some respects additional freedoms not enjoyed by other athletes by living in the dormitory I was originally assigned to live. The athletic dormitory experience worked out well in the end, and no official explanation was ever given for the original dormitory assignment. However, the situation was stressful for a teenager living away from home for the first time, from the start of the fall semester up to the transition to the new dormitory environment. Prior to the decision to permit me to live in the athlete's dormitory, it was odd following basketball practice and basketball games to see the other athletes go from the gymnasium to the dormitory located adjacent to the gymnasium, while I was required to go much farther up the hill to get to my dormitory.

On the days of basketball games out of town, while an athlete at Texas State University, there were times when it was very uncomfortable, as some restaurants and hotels would not entertain or serve the team so long as I was present. We had to move to different places to be served, once the managers of the establishments, restaurants, and hotels, were made aware that I was there as part of the basketball team. In one of the basketball games in Natchitoches, Louisiana I was the only person of color that I saw in the facility. The fans and players from the opposing team made unkind remarks and taunted me with insults during the game in full view and knowledge of the referees and other officials who permitted the abusive conduct and took no action for correction. My coaches and teammates, however, were supportive. My playing time in this game was short and uncomfortable, but I remained confident in my abilities and faith.

During my college experience, one of the most stressful situations was when I was required to have surgery in the lower back area for the removal of a cyst which had grown to be exceptionally large and bleeding. Following the surgery, I was required to wear diapers on my backside to prevent the bleeding onto my clothes. I was able to keep this matter a secret, but regardless it was uncomfortable for a brief stretch of time. I stayed away from other people to the extent practical. I also experienced two other major surgeries several years later while serving as a teacher and coach in Austin, both related to participation in athletics in earlier years: cartilage tear in the left leg (prior to the option for a laser procedure) and Achilles tendon, right leg. The Achilles tendon tear occurred during a fundraiser event where Austin coaches competed in a basketball game with players from the Dallas Cowboys football team. The Dallas players were big and strong and in good shape; I could not claim either of those advantages – not so big, not so strong, and certainly not in good shape. The subsequent surgery and recovery period were reminders that I am not invincible. I now look at this story as "old news". I decided to "Let it go!' Move on to the next issue.

The odd and uncomfortable experiences in traveling from city to city were not limited to the college experience. Family travel out of town while growing up was primarily limited to and from Bryan and Houston, Texas to visit relatives. Also, while in high school, I traveled to Waco, Dallas, and Fort Worth, as those cities were the closest places for our district basketball team competition for the Original L. C. Anderson High School (plus occasional competitions in Houston). Hotel options were limited, and I remember when we stopped at service stations for gasoline, there were typically separate water fountains for African Americans and White people to drink from due to Jim Crow standards. The full merger of the Prairie View Interscholastic League and University Interscholastic League occurred in 1970, starting the transition to integrated activities for some sports in 1966. Until that time the extracurricular activities were segregated by race.

In many instances my wife, Carolyn, and I have been stopped and searched at airports as travelers of color, where other travelers were not. I have the utmost respect for and appreciation of the police and military, although there are times when they are misrepresented by "rogue" officers, making it more difficult for everyone. In one situation at a Houston airport for example, I believed that I was disrespected by officers in full view of the family and others after going through the airport scanner while entering the boarding area, that is, facing body search -- pat down and being required to send personal items, such as my wallet, through the scanner a second time. The verbal abuse and disrespectful conduct by the police officers were disheartening. In another situation, Carolyn was not allowed to re-enter the United States upon being detained and required to distinguish herself from another Carolyn Brown following travel to Europe: London, England and Paris, France, by a flight originating in Houston, Texas, and transferring in Detroit on the way to Europe. We experienced a Eurostar train ride from London to Paris and returned to Texas from Charles De Gaulle Airport, with the first stop in Amsterdam, the Netherlands, then to Houston. The only place she or I experienced a problem was upon return to the United States in Houston at the airport. The officers at the entry station were rude, especially to Carolyn who was detained by immigration officers, requiring her to go to a back room without me for further review. There was no explanation given to her or to me, and they appeared to be offended that we would ask questions about the delay and procedure. An hour later after her detainment, she was cleared to leave, but only after being insulted by the experience and time wasted. Again, we began the trip in Houston, and each one of us had in our possession the appropriate credentials throughout the trip. A complaint was filed with the United States government, but responses received were generic, at best, and no apology was issued nor promise of disciplinary action to be imposed on those who violated our time and dignity. We decided after a brief period to remain focused upon the future and not the past and, therefore, "Let it go!" Move on to the next issue.

Far too many times in adulthood my family and I have been directed in restaurants to sit in the back of the restaurant, in the corner away from the front or middle where most people sit. Coincidence, perhaps so and perhaps not, but the perceived stigma and feelings of discomfort are sometimes difficult to ignore, especially, being knowledgeable of cases where people of color have been treated differently as customers of various establishments, due to race considerations.

In spite of the many years of success in achieving a consistent track record of success in standing tall in planning and providing leadership for putting conditions in place in support of children, I have encountered some challenges: controversies that were deliberately planted and personal attacks as part of "push back" against reform and change. In my work I have been strong in character and ethics, supportive of personnel and children and strongly involved with the community for greater success for the children. The reality of being in the role of change or "turnaround" agent has been the challenge of balancing the need to be friendly, easy to approach and personable with the need to demonstrate excellence in character and professionalism and holding self and others accountable for results. Another reality in "change agent" leadership is to acknowledge that not everyone wants to change and not everyone wants to experience transformation. They prefer to keep things just as is and will do anything to stop change, including attacking the persons in leadership who attempt to make things work better or differently for the common good. A leader also must acknowledge that not everyone is going to be for you or your success.

Interestingly, when faced with accusations and criticisms, the less said the better, and you can only hope that your "good name" and positive accomplishments will override the negative chatter and attacks which, unfortunately, come with the territory -- whether man or woman -- in leadership roles. It has been my desire and honor to serve as a leader in urban, poor communities because I believed that I could make a positive difference. I was fortunate to enjoy a background and experiences for development of unique qualifications as an education leader and "change agent". I am very proud of the accomplishments, especially when the record shows such dramatic success in environments where they had not experienced such success in the past: academics, finance, facilities; human resources; community and parental involvement and more. I have long held the view that there are times and places where somebody must "shake things up" for the better, and I would not trade the experience to do it any other way. After all, the children deserve it and, thereby, all can enjoy a better quality of life when we improve the conditions for learning.

I have learned through some controversies and growth experiences that you cannot count on everybody being for reform and change and for placing the common good above self-interest. It is better to run from these people to the extent that you can protect yourself and the projects of concern. While people can change, the reality is that it is more productive to spend your time on aligning yourself with a team of honorable, committed reformers who wish to work for what is important. Also, it is beneficial to keep a safe distance away from those who may not only work to block progress but who are willing to harm themselves or others just to get their way. It is understood the phrase of keeping enemies "close to you" so you know what they are up to, but what is more suitable in excellent leadership is to be more focused on the mission and remaining aligned with the team of reformers for the improvements desired. It is not necessary for everyone to like you anymore than it is important for you to like everyone else. It is the accomplishing of the mission and providing leadership to achieve the mission that is much more significant. Always keep in mind to save your trust only for those who earn it. Then "Let it go"! Move on to the next issue. I believed positive change could happen, and that is what I focused on. I have kept the faith – in things hoped for and the evidence of things not yet seen.

The concept of schooling, with part of the purpose being to serve the common good and promote democracy, makes so much sense. However, far too often I have found that what is most important to some people is not the common good but their own personal gain, or that of their friends and family when it comes to jobs, contracts, and accountability. "I want my way and I want it now" is not a foreign concept in schools or business organizations across the country, and this approach is quite commonly advanced over seeking what is the best decision or right for children. The persons who make attempts to do things the right way or "by the book" are often criticized as "the problem" or characterized as not being a team player. This issue is a problem at all levels, including some members of school boards, community members, parents, school personnel, business leaders, and, even, some government officials.

As an education leader in administration, there were many times when I faced challenges that were unique and difficult to address. The most difficult were those situations involving serious illness or death of employees or students. It was especially challenging when I either knew the person or family and when I was expected to comment, privately to the family and at funerals, representing the school districts in which

I worked. Being a caring person, I have vivid memories of those times when I had to share sad realities with families. I recall attending a funeral of a student whose name I did not know. As I entered the church service, the pastor called my name to come forward to make comments before I had the opportunity to review the service program. Fortunately, I was able to secure a program by lifting it from one of the mourners seated in the audience as I walked forward toward the podium, allowing me to personalize my remarks. In another example, I was asked to make comments at the funeral of one of the police officers in Birmingham, Alabama who was very well known by faculty, staff, and students of his assigned school -- an incredibly sad and challenging situation. One of the most difficult tasks that I performed occurred in Cleveland, Ohio, where I took the responsibility of contacting a parent whose child had deliberately jumped from a window to his death. Lastly, in March 2002, on the same day that I went to DeKalb County, Georgia, and signed a contract for employment there but was still working in Birmingham, Alabama, it was most touching and heartbreaking that a child in Birmingham was killed by a "drive by" shooter. The student was just standing there in a park along with many other young people who were attending a so-called Senior Skip Day. Many years later, I can recall arriving at the crime scene, after driving from Georgia back to Birmingham, to observe the child still lying on the ground. Children and parents remained nearby who were expressing their grief and anger. The shooter was identified and pleaded guilty to murder. However, the needless loss of that child will always be a disturbing memory burned into my mind. It was tough then, and now, as I reflect on what happened.

Admittedly, while I am so very pleased about the opportunities and my successes in education, while attending elementary school through college and working as teacher, coach, and leader in school districts, there remain some disappointments about not pursuing the dream of attending law school and seeking political office on a national basis. As a youngster, I had considered becoming a lawyer and devoting time and attention on pushing for change in civil and human rights for all. I decided to pursue such an agenda through education. While happy with the chosen career, the original approach was to pursue the civil and human rights agenda through preparation in law and working in the public, political arena. I have a lot to be proud of in working as an education leader in places facing challenging circumstances for promoting a "rights" agenda. I happen to believe things happen for a reason, and I am most pleased about the opportunity to serve in places where I have lived and worked. "Let it go!" Move on to the next issue. I have kept the faith.

The Emerson Street Story: Race, Class, Quality of Life and Faith is in large part a testimony about how growing up in such an environment proved to be most beneficial within and across all aspects of my life. I gained an extraordinary sense of meaning and the joy of living and direction, in terms of how to live a life of purpose and for demonstrating an advent attitude of hospitality in reaching out to help other people. I continue to search for and expect truth, meaning and understanding of and appreciation for purpose in all that I think and do.

Chapter Four

Well Tested and Foundation Strong

I was fortunate to grow up in a family environment the foundation of which was reminiscent of the biblical phrase, *"liken him unto a wise man, which built his house upon a rock"* (Matthew 7: 24). We faced challenges but none so severe as to tear through or even stretch the core of our family values or love and support of each other and our determination to serve the common good. We kept the faith – in things hoped for and the evidence of things not yet seen.

My family for generations has been engaged in church and influenced by faith-based principles in all that we think, say, and do. The concepts of serving others, reaching out to help friends, neighbors, and community, and treating others as "you would have others treat you" define our way of life. Such concepts are faith and spiritually based in nature and commonly stressed and practiced in our faith-based orientation and are part of the foundation, based upon which my family operates. We all make mistakes. Yet, in growing up my family elders, church members, and other adults in the community stressed these ideals, with special emphasis on doing that which we may to help self, family, and others to enjoy a better quality of life. We also learned the importance of following the law and being loyal to family and working hard in employment each day. Our family for many generations has routinely practiced the principles of the Winners Always Practice

Program, which are summarized in a later chapter in this book. We learned the best way to rebound from mistakes is to acknowledge them and follow up by reversing them with corrections.

No doubt there have been struggles along the way for family and those around us. Yet, the foundation upon which our values are based has enabled my birth family and in-laws to weather the "storms" with grace and to move forward in enjoying life to the fullest extent, even with the moderate resources at our disposal. Such an attitude has been nicely aligned with our faith and our practiced determination to succeed. The elders in the family lived according to extremely limited options and resources, with opportunities limited by race and class considerations. They persevered through the difficult economic times and worked hard in their "common laborer" jobs and encouraged the youth to become educated and work hard, so that we would be poised to take advantage of opportunities before us. Becoming educated was a key variable in the formula for improving circumstances for the family. My birth family also actively reached out to help other people of all races, faiths, and backgrounds. It was not unusual during my growth and development to have friends of differing races and backgrounds visit from outside the neighborhood. Carolyn and I are proud and thankful that our children have learned and demonstrated the same understanding of those concepts of appreciating diversity, as is evident from observing their friends and acquaintances in elementary and secondary grade school, college and beyond. Our family is an excellent living model of the results of faith, becoming educated, working hard, and of enjoying the advantages for appreciating people of all races and backgrounds. When faced with struggles or difficulties, what matters more than where you start is where you end up. We are boastful that our model is an excellent one for showing what high quality of life looks and feels like, through the lens formed of both setbacks and victories.

The successes enjoyed by our children are in no way a surprise or unexpected. Carolyn and I were deliberate in selecting the schools they attended and, in some cases, the teachers. We spent time with our son and daughters in attending school programs and visiting with faculty and staff, and we made it a practice to have regular conversations with our children about each of their school days. We also have been consistent -- up to and including today -- that when our son and daughters have called or wanted a moment to talk, we have answered, no matter how busy our day or night may be going. We shared in the experience of working through a difficult grade school or college assignment, making sure they took the responsibility to complete their own work. We attended church as a family on a regular basis, initially, in St. Peter's United Methodist Church in Austin, Texas, and currently at the Antioch Missionary Baptist Church in Beaumont, Texas. We routinely went on outings such as picnics and enjoyed family vacations in popular amusement venues. Some of the time it was unreasonably cool, windy, or too hot for comfort during our picnic outings, but we did attempt to spend quality time together whenever we could. We took the time to teach things like how to ride a bicycle, and we encouraged them to read. Each of them enjoyed experiences with extracurricular activities, such as baseball and football teams and band for our son, and basketball team and band for our youngest daughter, and basketball, tennis, dance, and band for our oldest daughter. All three also participated in various other school organizations. Yet, in hindsight despite our jobs, which could at times be demanding on our time, looking back I only wish we could have spent even more quality time during our children's growth and developmental years. Today, we make it a practice to communicate with our son and two daughters routinely.

The influence on me from my grandparents was strong, especially on my mother's side, through visits and communication with them in Bryan, Texas, my mother's birth home. The love and concern they demonstrated for their grandchildren and their children, including my mother, was always strong and consistent. The house they lived in was modest and located in a rural area. The house was lacking in terms of what is commonly found in houses today, for example, no washing machine and dryer, and the toilet was an outhouse located a few feet from the house. On the paternal side, I knew well my grandfather who would visit from time to time. However, I was not able to enjoy much time with my paternal grandmother, as she died during the time of my early childhood.

My school and career plans were deliberately designed for maximum exposure to and interactions with specified people and included taking advantage of those circumstances that would better enable me to make a positive difference. For example, in attending the Texas State University, the experience was positive overall, and I grew professionally and completed the requirements for the Bachelor of Science in Education and Master of Education degrees, successfully and with honor. I can still remember the first night at the school away from my Austin home as I stood on the dormitory balcony looking around the campus. It was a strange and somewhat frightening experience but also enlightening.

While in attendance at the school as an undergraduate student, there were some memorable moments and some challenges. Most were positive but some were not. On the positive side, the coaches, professors, and fellow students were friendly and supportive, overall, and I became better educated. On the other hand, there were some unfortunate occurrences that made the university experience uncomfortable and tense. For example, there were instances of hazing -- "warmups" -- where the upper classmen would impose sanctions as they chose. When a freshman student could not answer a question about personal or family specifics, such as where an upper-class athlete was born or where their parents were born or the age of a sister, brother or parent, sanctions would follow. Questions were designed for the freshman students to answer incorrectly. We were asked to sit on rulers and directed not to fall off within a specified amount of time. The consequences of failing the tests included swats with a board on the buttocks and other forms of degrading actions. If we resisted, the consequences would carry over into the following day during formal team practice and beyond, with coaching staff being on site to view or witness, and even accepting, such behavior under the umbrella of "team building". These activities were part of the history or fabric of the athletic program and not easily questioned by anyone, especially the freshman students. These practices were questionable and wrong in many cases; although, they appeared to be intended to grow the group toward a common bond of appreciation for one another -- not intended to harm in any way.

In another specific example of hazing, the freshman basketball team players were awakened early one dark morning, blindfolded and driven away to the woods several miles away, somewhere in an area near Wimberley, Texas (about 15 miles) and left to find our way back to the dormitory. Fortunately, one of my teammates had money and paid a hog farmer who owned a truck and was traveling in the woods to give us a ride, covering most of the distance back to the school. Freshman students were required to "sport" a large "T" for SWTSU (college name letters) cut into our hair, bald around the "T". Coaches allowed and even spoke with us to encourage us to "go along to get along", even relating to the teasing which sometimes was "sprinkled" with racially insensitive type jokes -- like differences in hair texture and more. I persevered and completed the "course", but not without some instances of discomfort and tense moments. The athletic director and head coach and assistant coach were supportive, overall, while making attempts to help all concerned to get along and appreciate each other as teammates.

The undergraduate experience was mostly positive with teammates and coaches. College professors and classes were pleasant. There was much media attention due to my status as the first African American athlete at the school. With respect to the cafeteria experience on campus, most of the time in the early years of my four undergraduate years, there was no one else of color in the room. There were also some unkind and uncomfortable situations on some game trips in Texas and in Louisiana at basketball games on those occasions where the restaurants and hotels did not serve the team due to my being there. Those restaurants and hotels had policies and practices of segregation that caused the denial of service to the entire team because I was an African American member of the team.

Imagine traveling from San Marcos, Texas, to another city in Texas or Louisiana, and when arriving at a restaurant to eat or hotel to spend the night, you observe some conversation occurring out of "ear shot" but where it appears those speaking with the coaches are staring toward you. Moments later, the team is then informed that we must leave to go to another restaurant or hotel, learning later that the reason is because the establishment would not serve the team because I was a part of it. It was a devastating experience and memorable in a profound way, serving as a spark for interest in providing leadership for needed change and for writing about it in hopes that others will not experience the same. One goal is to remind us all how far we have moved forward and how important it is that we remain vigilant not to repeat those mistakes in human behavior. My thoughts at the time were consistent with my current thinking -- the glass is full and overflowing. Let us replace it with a taller glass. We can and should continue opening the door to look for new and improved ways to look beyond race and toward a movement for making the quality of life better for all.

In furthering my education through completion of the terminal degree, I was most fortunate to complete doctoral studies and graduate from The University of Texas at Austin. The support of one of my mentors, Dr. Nolan Estes, made a tremendous difference in the application process, as he was at the time the leader of the prestigious Cooperative Superintendents Program, of which I was selected to participate. I am also grateful to the entire dissertation committee, chaired by Dr. Lonnie H. Wagstaff. It was most exhilarating to earn the Doctor of Philosophy Degree, the dissertation title of which is <u>Leader Behavior and School Effectiveness</u>. The focus of the study was on school principals' leadership for guiding two processes identified in effective schools' research: instructional leadership and positive home-school relations in urban minority high schools, copyright, 1991.

The college classroom experience from the first year through doctoral studies was important and worthwhile, and the exposure to highly respected writers, researchers, and professors from around the world was even more special. The professors for doctoral studies and dissertation were well prepared and supportive, including the chairman, Dr. Lonnie Wagstaff, and Drs. I. Carl Candoli, Jay D. Scribner, Michael P. Thomas. Jr., and Walter E. Jordan-Davis, a professional colleague who also served on the dissertation committee. The cooperation among students and faculty was mutually respectful and collegial. The percentage of students of color at The University of Texas was much lower than the population of White students. The University has since then made attempts to become more progressive and inclusive of students and faculty of color and become more up to date in its policies, procedures, and practices. This is, of course, after many years of being un-progressive and more restrictive in its policies and actions regarding race considerations. Applause is well deserved for the departments and programs in place today where the focus is dedicated toward addressing issues on community engagement and diversity. Also, there has been positive movement in athletics in the hiring of coaches of color and women in major sports programs.

Carolyn and I faced a different kind of challenge in the form of a major hurricane while living in Southeast Texas, Hurricane Harvey. The storm struck most directly in our area, August 29, 2017, with heavy winds and a record amount of rainfall of over 60 inches of rain. Our house was flooded with over three feet of water throughout the house. We were fortunate to have an upstairs "bonus" room to go to for Carolyn, our Chihuahua pet and myself for safety. It was an amazing and frightful storm. It rained incessantly, seemingly at the time to never stop. The local roads and highways, including Interstate Highway 10 and U. S. Highway 69 were closed due to flooding, and the local hotels experienced heavy flooding as well. Even the local convention center and library experienced major flooding. The convention center had been set up as a safe-place shelter, but those who had gone there for safety had to be evacuated due to flooding inside the facility. Inside our house we lost many of our belongings, including furniture, clothes, appliances, books, and outside two automobiles, and more. We were able to save much of the computer technology. In fact, with all the fearful conditions and excitement, one of the first priorities was to take the computers upstairs to safe territory.

We mistakenly thought we could block the water from entering the house by placing towels and throw rugs in front of the front and back doors. We learned by early evening that such a battle strategy would not work, as we saw water beginning to build up inside our bedrooms, coming up through the carpet flooring. It was over at that point and time to save all we could before going upstairs. Interestingly, the electricity remained on until we turned off the breaker as a safety measure.

Fortunately, one of our neighbors was able to rely on friends who lived outside the hurricane danger zone who were willing to travel to our neighborhood in a boat to move us to safety. This husband and wife team was most generous with their time and efforts to move several families out of the flood zone to the local bowling alley, which served as an emergency transfer station. Our boat and several others docked there, unloading those who had been moved from the flooded area toward safety. Then upon arrival we were escorted by a pick-up truck to a local church serving as a care shelter, where they were set up to receive upwards of a hundred evacuees. They were genuinely nice and well prepared to assist with dry clothes of all sizes; food; drinks; sleeping cots; animal cages; and more. It was a beautiful picture of positive helping hands for those in need of assistance. It was equally as beautiful to observe people of differing races and backgrounds coming together to "hold hands" in a moment of crisis and the joy of being saved from the storm conditions -- no "big I's and little u's", a real-life experience of unity. We kept the faith – in things hoped for and the evidence of things not yet seen. Indeed, this situation was a test of our faith.

We were not able to return to our neighborhood until nearly a week later, where the process began of moving out the damaged property and salvaging what we could. There had been so many boats (over 100) which came into the neighborhood to save residents, the water force damaged our garage door, so much so that we had to replace it as we worked to repair our home.

We remained overnight in the shelter and were fortunate to secure a hotel room the following night, much luckier than many others. We stayed in local hotels until the end of December, moving from one hotel to another due to availability and other considerations. The United States government, through the Federal Emergency Management Agency (FEMA), was extremely helpful to us throughout the process, especially upon their establishing a management system to communicate with us and the thousands of others who needed assistance. One of the huge benefits we enjoyed was the provision of a portable trailer, which was delivered by the government to our home area open space lot; we were fortunate to own the property next to our home upon which the trailer was delivered. We remained in the trailer while the work on our house proceeded until February 2019, a year and a half after the hurricane. Not all were so fortunate to enjoy such a facility for residence. We were also fortunate and wise to have purchased home flood and windstorm insurance since the homeowner's insurance did not apply to the situation. We were wise to maintain a relationship with the contractor whose company built the house, and he was available to orchestrate the recovery efforts; albeit, along with the other 37 hurricane properties his company had contracted with to repair. Our experience with Hurricane Harvey was a humbling experience, but through it all we felt blessed.

Chapter Five

Impact of Schooling and General Work Experiences

A person is greatly influenced by the environment in which he or she grows up and operates, including the influences of the home, spiritual community, travel exposure, community, and work environment. Many, many experiences helped to lay the strong foundation upon which I now proudly stand. Such experiences, in large part, were the result of planning and anticipated opportunities. Although, some of the activities enjoyed came about by unexpected circumstances and were not so well planned.

My school experiences from elementary through high school in Austin, Texas and my earning the Bachelor of Science in Education and Master of Education Degrees at Texas State University and earning the Doctor of Philosophy Degree at The University of Texas at Austin were all profound and memorable. I was fortunate to enjoy excellence and success throughout my educational experiences in elementary school through college, at all levels and at all schools. Also, I was fortunate to be supported by family, teachers, and colleagues who "reached out" to guide and encourage me beyond ordinary and without considerations of race. I was delighted to earn the opportunity to serve as head basketball coach at what then was the "new" high school in Austin, Texas, for which the school name was the same as my high school years, the Original L. C. Anderson High School, although in a different part of town. The opening of this high school was in the Northwest Hills area of Austin and was history making because the naming of this "new" school was part of efforts by the school district leadership to assuage the concerns of those who had attended the school of the same name, located in East Austin and closed due to the plans to desegregate schools. The principal of the school was formerly a teacher at the original high school who later became well respected for his work as an educator and community representative. Some of the teachers were chosen from the original high school as well. The "new" Anderson High School was an icon of integration measures being put into practice in the city. The opening of the "new" high school was intended to reflect excellence at the highest levels and to demonstrate what integration in education should look like, as students from the immediate, largely White neighborhood and African American students bused from across town would attend.

There were challenges during my grade school years, and the opportunities for learning in the public schools in Austin were routinely inequitable from elementary through high school, due to policies and historical practices related to race and school segregation. New books? No. Never was I issued a new book from elementary through high school, and books were "worn" and "handed down" to us from the White race schools after those schools had discarded them. School facilities were not as nice as the other schools "across town", and the equipment was not up to date and too often not operable. I never experienced attending a new or renovated school. All my public education experiences occurred in segregated African American schools. Teachers were nice, caring, and dedicated professionals; however, they sometimes lacked appropriate training and preparation. Yet, discipline management was handled very well, and the school environment was pleasant in each school I attended. The classes in high school were organized through a tracking design just as many schools of today, where only designated students were exposed to the top curriculum. Therefore, only some students were exposed to advanced coursework such as calculus and physics. I was, unfortunately, not selected to be one of those so privileged to enjoy exposure to the top-level curriculum.

My education experiences in college were positive but were limited by the lack of adequate preparation in public grade school, lack of exposure to the top curriculum, and due to the realities of the use of outdated learning materials during those years. The college entrance examination results were affected by the level of instruction leading up to those exams, both for entry into undergraduate and graduate level schools. For example, upon enrollment into The University of Texas doctoral program at Austin in courses such as statistics, no doubt the background and lack of exposure in previous studies impaired my preparation for the classes. No excuses. Therefore, I simply had to work harder and put in longer hours to be able to perform well. I maintained an attitude of determination and confidence that if others can do it, so can I. I kept the faith -- in things hoped for and the evidence of things not yet seen.

The undergraduate work and athletics experiences at Texas State University were memorable in terms of coursework and participation in athletics -- basketball player and first African American athlete at the school during the mid-1960s for any sport. I was an average to good student and athlete as an undergraduate student in college. The professors were knowledgeable in their subjects, as well as friendly and generally effective in delivery of instruction. The coaches and the other players on the basketball team were friendly and supportive. Initially, the coaches were concerned about whether I was prepared to pursue a degree in government -- pre-law focus, suggesting instead that I pursue a degree in physical education. While I did earn the degree with physical education as my major field, I completed the requirements for a degree in political science/government as my minor field of study, because I continued my interest in pursuing a career in law. I was convinced that I would succeed despite fears and concerns expressed by coaches and others upon entering college. The students in college within and outside athletics were supportive and positive. Although, there were times when I found myself in the unwelcomed position of having to inform some students not to make me the "butt" of teasing or jokes linked to racial stereotyping statements. They were making conversation, but racial jokes were uncomfortable for me; I preferred other topics.

While working to complete the doctorate, one of the key professors and mentors at The University of Texas at Austin was there at every turn for giving support, as part of the Cooperative Superintendency Program, looking beyond race considerations to demonstrate support and encouragement - Dr. Nolan Estes. I was most encouraged by the experiences and continue to prosper because of them. Indeed, it is true that one teacher can make a huge difference in education, on behalf of children and adults. I believed before and continue to believe in the concept: the glass is full and overflowing; let us replace it with a taller glass. That is, we should do what we can to come up with new ideas to make the quality of life better for those who aspire to learn and grow like me and, indeed, all of us. We should spend more of our time looking for ways to open the doors of opportunities for people of all races and creeds and not take time to block anyone.

In career experiences and progression from the start to finish, I enjoyed success in serving children, from self-preparation to putting conditions in place to achieve documented records of positive outcomes for students' academic achievement -- developing the whole child. Prior to serving as superintendent, my job progress and success appeared not to be dramatically limiting or restricted by race or any other issues. I was proud to hold several jobs with success, such as playground supervisor for the Austin Area Parks and Recreation Department, where I was part of a team to ensure that conditions were safe and fun for visitors, including serving as coach of the men's softball team. I thoroughly enjoyed the job of teacher-coach in San Antonio and Austin, Texas, and becoming the first African American principal at O. Henry Middle School in Austin. I was so honored and proud, as several public officials' children attended. Parents included, for example, the school district board president, Governor of the State of Texas, former Comptroller for the State of Texas, United States Congressman, and other state officials. I also enjoyed serving as director of student support programs and other roles in the Austin Independent School District. In addition, I proudly served as the deputy superintendent in Cleveland, Ohio, and executive deputy superintendent in Houston, Texas. Following these experiences,

I was named as superintendent in four locations: first, as superintendent in Metro-Dallas (Wilmer-Hutchins), Texas; and later in Birmingham, Alabama; DeKalb County, Georgia; and Port Arthur, Texas. In DeKalb County I was the first African American superintendent selected, and just about every issue or decision appeared to be connected to or affected by considerations of race and class. In all the school districts where I worked as superintendent, the composition of students was predominately students of color. Two of these school districts were managed before my tenure by the State of Texas, due to issues with student performance, finance, and governance: Wilmer-Hutchins (metro-Dallas area) and Port Arthur, upon my entering each School District -- otherwise commonly called state takeover. In both situations I was recruited by the state education agency and school districts as superintendent to provide leadership to help "turn things around". Upon departure from both districts the data clearly reflected success in raising achievement, balancing the budget, dramatically improving facilities and revamping procedures and operations for smoother relations among the administration and the school board. In Port Arthur, for example, we accomplished some incredible things: in terms of achievement great improvements were made; finance -- increased reserves and balanced the budget; facilities -- advanced technology, built new schools and renovated all other schools; and, we dramatically increased the involvement of parents and community.

The work in Cleveland, Ohio, was special. The environment was full of politics, that is, seven personnel union bargaining units and school board communications which were often contentious, inside, and outside of school board meetings. For example, there was one meeting where the principals' union decided to publicly wage a fight against an administrative decision on the formula for assigning the number of assistant principals to schools; they wanted to increase the number. With no advance notification provided to the superintendent or me, the deputy superintendent, principals marched into the school board committee meeting as a show of force to make their opinions known to school board members and to the administration. The school board members who attended the meeting had received advance notification of the principals' plans to protest at the meeting. The school district was struggling at the time with the budget, facing a deficit of over $70 million dollars. The district had requested support from the public to raise the tax millage, but the public had refused such requests in partial response to their displeasure about the decisions on desegregation of schools which had occurred many years prior. In one budget saving action, the school board called an emergency meeting and voted to lay off all early childhood teachers. Neither the superintendent nor I, as deputy superintendent, was notified of the meeting until after the meeting was held. The school district treasurer, however, was made aware and participated in the meeting.

In all the school districts where I worked in leadership roles, there were patterns and evidence of micro-management by school board members and other public officials in governing, and we were affected by the politics of education which either promoted or limited our progress. The focus was routinely taken away from the priorities of the established mission and goals of the school districts. Was I always right and were they always wrong? No. I, however, made efforts to focus all decisions on the impact on children and their best interests. Birmingham, for example, was identified as the school district with the highest number of schools in Alabama on the low academic performance list prior to my tenure as superintendent, representing one-third of the schools in Alabama on the list. By the time of my departure, the district had no schools on the low performance list, as schools made dramatic academic improvements. We also made dramatic improvements in finance and capital improvement projects, and we reduced the list of concerns on the state finance audit to practically none and made dramatic improvements in building new schools and renovating others. Yet, the most profound challenges before and during my tenure in Birmingham were related to lack of resources and the politics of education. More specifically, at the start, there were serious issues regarding governance in terms of school board and superintendent relationships and lack of employee accountability. There were other challenges where the employee association (union) made unrealistic demands, and they successfully pushed for state legislation and policies which protected employees from requirements to perform. Such limitations and disruptions led by the employee association were based upon the strength of the association in alignment with state officials, as the organization represented the largest political action program in the entire state. Yet, the individuals associated with membership and leadership in the organization were friendly and seemed willing to discuss important issues.

As superintendent in every district where I worked, we made dramatic improvements in academics, finance, facilities, and increased involvement of the community, business, and parents, and we made deliberate efforts to better engage higher education institutions. In DeKalb County, Georgia, for example, we proudly made double-digit gains in test scores and dramatically increased the number of schools achieving state, district, and federal standards. Such improvements were made regardless of the initial challenges forced by budget concerns. The district expenditures exceeded revenues received for four of the six years prior to my arrival and the district had only a couple of weeks of revenues in reserves at the start of my tenure. We reduced spending by $45 million dollars in one year and $7 million the following year, which included reassignment of more than 20 central office administrators to school level vacant positions – not "happy campers", indeed. We persevered and continued to raise standards and test scores and successfully managed the $500 million Special Purpose Local Option Sales Tax (SPLOST) capital bond program, which voters approved during the time of my transition to the DeKalb County school district from another district. In Port Arthur we also made double digit gains in test scores and balanced the budget as well as increased reserves and passed a capital bond program, which enabled the district to build new schools and renovate all others. We were able to rather swiftly convince State of Texas Officials to move out of the district from its position of state takeover, the situation which had been in operation for 18 months prior to my arrival. A similar story of successful leadership had also taken place in a school district in the Metro-Dallas area (Wilmer-Hutchins) where I also served as superintendent.

In review of my schooling and work experiences, I have enjoyed many opportunities for molding my own attitudes and view of life and people, in general. I would not trade any of them, even if given the chance. I especially enjoyed the experience of being a coach in athletics. My teams performed very well in each role as coach. We won first place for the seventh-grade basketball championship and second place in football in San Antonio during my first year on the job. I was also proud to enjoy success as the first L. C. Anderson High School head basketball coach with a season record of 24 wins and 6 losses during our best year; in that season we had a district-wide posting of 15 wins and 1 loss. In addition, I was named Coach of the Year by my peers in Austin during that year. The players I coached have enjoyed much success beyond high school sports as adults. My success in coaching was based upon similar principles I stressed in education leadership: high expectations, strong discipline and character, excellent planning and organization, routine skill development, emphasis on teamwork, and accountability stressed among players and coaches.

Beyond teaching and coaching jobs, I genuinely enjoyed serving in an administrative capacity in education. The role of superintendent was one of the most enjoyable work experiences. The role of principal was pleasurable and positive, as well. I deliberately decided to work as leader in urban, mostly low-income communities which had not enjoyed a sustained record of success. There were some common themes identified in these communities: resistance to change, even if the change would clearly be better for students and the common good; micro-management by several members of the school board and other public officials; low expectations by employees, parents, community, and students; lack of preparation and planning for success; resistance to holding employees accountable for results; poor teaching practices among teachers; limited and inequitable resources and not properly aligned with what is good for the children; lenient student management practices; lack of focus on understanding and implementation of the curriculum; conditions and environment not suitable for student success; low parental and community involvement; and the politics of education which appeared to overwhelm and distract from what matters most. By working in such circumstances and due to my actions to push for change and reform, I faced criticism, which was often unfair and irrational. At times I faced personal attacks on my "good name" and character as a tactic for distracting me from "working on the work" for children.

I have continued to press forward, in spite of the challenges and criticisms, and I feel encouraged that, although, the "glass" can be looked upon as half full or "full" or even overflowing, in terms of progress, a "taller glass" continues to be in order. That conceptualization gives more room and space in our thoughts and our drive to take actions for continuation of progress in schools and in reaching for a high quality of life for all. There is always room for improvement in any school system. Part of the daily struggles and joys associated with superintendent leadership is balancing between doing what is the "right" thing to do in decision making with the need to get along with and follow the will of the school board and others. There are times when making the right decision may result in alienating many including, but not limited to, the governing board, whose members are in the position to supervise, hire and terminate the superintendent. It can really get interesting if the decision has to do with the areas of personnel, vendor contracts, and selection of programs to use or not to use. I have been reminded more than once that when making personnel decisions, each person affected, directly or indirectly, has relatives or friends, who never go away. Sometimes they remain angry for life, and, therefore, they become and remain your enemy and may or may not let you know, openly. Yet, the best decision is always to be focused on what is in the best interest of the children, ethically and lawfully, and to remain "high road" and positive in explaining to all concerned the position taken, and to let the "chips fall where they may".

Examples follow with respect to the politics of education which I have encountered in leadership while facing challenges and opportunities for doing the right thing on behalf of the children and, thereby, the common good for all concerned. These comments are provided as general summaries only and not intended to express details for the whole story, noting some repetition in portrayals that appeared earlier in the text.

Chapter Six

Politics of Education - DO THE "RIGHT THING"—EVERYTIME, EVERYDAY!

EXAMPLES FOLLOW ON THE POLITICS OF EDUCATION PER SCHOOL DISTRICT WHILE SERVING AS EDUCATION LEADER-SUPERINTENDENT

<u>Cleveland, Ohio</u> – Deputy Superintendent for Educational Programs. Transitioned back to Texas to join family, once Carolyn assumed a principalship in Austin, Texas. <u>70,000 Students.</u>

I often reflect on a narrative that occurred early in my tenure in Cleveland, Ohio. The superintendent was out of town, and I was the highest ranked employee on site. This scenario was noted earlier regarding the effect of union activities in an education environment. Unknown to me and other central office administrators, the school principals, under the umbrella of union action, marched into a school board education committee meeting to protest the formula for the number of assistant principals per school. The union group's intent to appear at the meeting obviously had been coordinated with the school board committee members. Even though no action was taken that day by the school board members, it was a highly unusual and questionable way to address the issue. In leadership for excellence in progress and results, it is important to practice this concept: "Let it go!" Move on to the next issue. "No harm – no foul" was my attitude, and the positive relationship enjoyed with the administrators did not change, because of the situation.

In Cleveland there were seven employee unions, and, regrettably, the superintendent and I spent hours in negotiations with them over various issues of concern. The union contract favored employees in certain circumstances over what was best for children and the teaching and learning process, such as, strict limit on time allotted for faculty meetings. If the meeting lasted one minute over that allotted time, teachers were encouraged by the union to walk out of the meeting, no matter the importance of the topic. There appeared to be no interest in the union leadership to hold instructional staff accountable for results in academic achievement.

In another example of politics over what is appropriate, the school board refused to consider a recommendation by the superintendent to select a fine arts supervisor during a regular school board meeting. Any school board member could block proposed recommendations. In this case, the one member who objected to the nomination did so because of a situation from prior years relating to a program that was held at the church his family attended, and the person nominated was the coordinator of that event. The member provided the explanation later, saying that so long as he served as a member of the school board, he would block that person from any promotion in administration. Again, the education leaders in administration were reminded to "Let it go!" Move on to the next issue.

The school board could call a meeting at a moment's notice, with or without consultation with the superintendent. The school board called an emergency meeting one day and voted to terminate all early childhood teachers as a cost saving measure. The school district was always under a threat of default, and we operated in a deficit budgetary mode throughout my tenure there -- as high as $70 million dollars in the "red" prior to and during my tenure. Any increase in the budget revenues required a vote by the public on the millage rate. Increases were routinely rejected by the public due primarily to their displeasure for many years about forced busing, as related to desegregation plans required by the federal government. We knew to "Let it go!" Move on to the next issue. Get the job done with less.

Under the superintendent's leadership, we implemented a program that was called Vision 21. We engaged the community and school employees in a citywide conversation about what we wanted schools to look like and how to increase student performance. School leaders and community leaders were tasked with agreeing on a school theme or approach and align the school operations with that approach to teaching and learning. For example, in the school where Carolyn was school principal, the approach selected was a comprehensive reform model termed Afrocentric Education. The curriculum and instruction for the students, most of whom were African American, included the children's experiences and was based upon their history, culture, and lineage. Student performance was dramatically improved through the Vision 21 program, led by the superintendent, Dr. Sammie Campbell Parrish.

* * *

Houston Independent School District – **Executive Deputy Superintendent for Educational Programs and Supervision of Schools. Also, responsible for 12 District Superintendents. Moved to the Wilmer-Hutchins Independent School District upon being recruited by the Texas Education Agency and Wilmer-Hutchins Independent School District School Board. 214,000 Students.**

The Honorable Dr. Rod Paige was selected as superintendent in 1994, while serving as a school board member in the Houston Independent School District. He had served as a school board member from 1989 to the time of his selection as superintendent. Prior to the assignment as superintendent, Dr. Paige formerly served for ten years as the dean of the School of Education at Texas Southern University. Dr. Paige was named United States Secretary of Education in 2001 as part of the cabinet of President George W. Bush. Since he had served as a colleague of school board members prior to becoming the superintendent, the communication overall with the other members of the school board was uniquely positive and cordial.

In the early 1990s, Dr. Paige and Dr. Don McAdams, a fellow school board member, co-authored the district's Declaration of Beliefs and Visions. In cooperation with the school board, they crafted a mission statement that included four essential points:

- HISD exists to support the relationship between the teacher and the student.
- HISD must decentralize.
- HISD must focus on performance, not compliance.
- HISD must require a common core of academic subjects for all students.

Under Dr. Paige's leadership, we implemented the Peer Examination, Evaluation, and Redesign (PEER) program. Through the PEER program, the administration invited business and community professionals to share ideas for improving the district's school support programs and services. The district also implemented a performance contract and incentive pay initiative, which entailed increases in pay for instructional personnel based upon performance. The 12 district superintendents were offered increased compensation of thousands of dollars for trade of one-year contracts over their original multi-year contracts. The district also implemented charter schools under the district's umbrella as part of its efforts to decentralize its operations, emphasizing more flexibility for schools in staffing and purchase of textbooks and materials.

We were proud of and thankful for the increases in student achievement at the elementary, middle school and high school levels. Among other programs that made a positive difference, implementation of the comprehensive approach in the teaching of reading was a huge impact. The administration designated a team of instructional specialists to work with a team of professors at the University of Houston to conduct research on the topic, and we designed a "train-the-trainer" staff development model, so that the results of our research could be spread widely among the instructional personnel across the school district. The reading test scores rivaled those of high-performing urban school systems across the nation because the students' reading test scores were so impressive.

The superintendent and his top executive level cabinet utilized data based upon multiple factors which may affect student learning improvement, such as student dropout and attendance rates, graduation statistics, and test scores in mathematics and reading per grade level, per school and per teacher within each school. When we observed gaps within and across classrooms, we explored reasons why. The results of such observations led to face-to-face meetings between principals, classroom teachers, and me on what may be causing low student test performance. The most severe consequences for poor instructional personnel performance was termination. In some cases, the conferences with the principals or teachers ended with their being relieved of their duty at the school(s), depending upon factors such as performance over time, degree to which employee development options had been explored, employee attendance and other similar factors. These conferences were held with principals, teachers, and district superintendents as part of our strict accountability approach. Pending determination of the final job action, the employee would be sent to a non-teaching position in the district's warehouse, not to return to the original assignment.

There were some awkward moments when the politics of education interfered with our intentions to do good work. One example was the occasion of a meeting with school board members, the superintendent, school personnel and me in a ceremony outdoors where a makeshift stage was set up and a curtain covered the wall behind it. There was no access to leave except to walk down the stairs which led to the podium. One of the school board members was upset about a comment that one of the speakers had made, and she attempted to leave the stage by going behind the curtain to exit the scene. The problem was that behind the stage there was no place to go because the curtain covered a concrete wall. Rather than return from behind the curtains to the stage and leave by walking down the steps in front, she chose to remain behind the curtain throughout the program, which lasted another 30 – 40 minutes.

In another awkward moment as the school district's executive deputy superintendent, I was proud to take the place of the superintendent for a program which he was unable to attend. Several school board members attended the program. During my remarks I was asked to introduce the school board members who were present, including the school board president. I did announce his name but did not acknowledge that he was the school board president. He later made it known that he was not pleased about what he considered to be a slight of his position of importance. I did apologize and moved on. "Let it go!" Move on to the next issue, but I did learn from the experience and did not make that mistake again for the remainder of my career as an education leader.

From time to time the school board members engaged in serious conversations about roles and responsibilities. If, for example, the superintendent had received a report from an employee or other source that a school board member had inserted himself or herself into communications about personnel or contract matters outside the regular process, he would raise the issue in front of the full board of trustees for review and response. He would do so in a calm, respectful manner, including confronting the individual school board member with a question whether he had their permission to raise the issue with the other school members. Tense moments? Yes, but professionally handled and productive in the long run, as such a practice helped by demonstration of what could happen when a school board member operated outside the regularly agreed upon procedures. The communications overall among the superintendent and school board members were cordial and professional, albeit at times tense and direct.

* * *

Wilmer-Hutchins Independent School District – Superintendent. Moved upon recruitment by officials in Birmingham, Alabama to become superintendent for that school district. 3,200 Students.

The Wilmer-Hutchins School District was under state management control by the Texas Education Agency upon my selection as the superintendent, and the state education regulation agency participated in my selection process. The school district had experienced problems with governance, facilities management, budget and finance and academics. I was serving in the Houston Independent School District as the Executive Deputy Superintendent for Educational Programs upon my selection as superintendent in Wilmer-Hutchins. Given the circumstances with state control, I had only a couple of days for transition and travel once the selection was made. In addition to the problems cited by the state, the school district had also experienced problems with federal government oversight regarding management of federal dollars intended for student programs. A few days prior to my beginning the work in the school district, the federal government conducted a raid where they seized school and bank records and office files. They also seized the office computers and locked every employee out of the building during the raid. There was no report on findings or concerns by the federal government from that episode at any time of my tenure. The school district was closed several years following my departure and was merged into a neighboring school district. The administration understood to practice the concept: "Let it go!" Move on to the next issue.

On one occasion, we experienced quite an emergency on payroll day when the bank and school district had not communicated about a bank account from which funds would be drawn for payroll related to coding numbers at the bottom of the payroll checks. Checks across the district "bounced" when employees attempted to cash them. The problem was not related to the revenues in place to cover payroll; lack of funds was not the issue. Therefore, we were able to correct the situation swiftly but not without much stress experienced by the employees. We had to do an extraordinary job for notifying employees and others as part of correcting the situation. We were faced with another excellent reminder of the need to "Let it go!" Move on to the next issue.

Everyone is concerned about their safety. Yet, fortunately not everyone has had to experience a situation such as I and the other central office employees experienced one evening when the sound of gunshots rang loudly inside the building. The shots were so powerful and impactful, the bullets pierced the outside door and traveled through the hallway to the next door and pierced a hole in that door as well at the far end of the hallway away from the first impact. The police were not able to identify the person responsible, but it did leave an eerie feeling among those of us at work at the time and beyond when working at night. Yet, another reminder of the need to think in terms of: "Let it go!" Move on to the next issue. Fortunately, no one was injured, and it turned out to be an isolated incident. We decided afterwards to leave the building earlier from that point, moving forward.

There were concerns expressed by state officials that previous district leaders had done favors for school board members, including making direct payments to the members for certain voting actions and that the contract bidding procedures were not followed appropriately. No concrete information was available or formal charges made by the state officials during my tenure in the school district or afterwards.

* * *

Birmingham City Schools, Alabama – **Superintendent. Moved to become superintendent in DeKalb County, Georgia. 38,000 Students.**

A former employee approached a school board member prior to a school board meeting and made a claim that the administrators of one of our high schools had coordinated a scheme in coordination with central office administrators to keep some students out of school on test days in hopes that the scores for the school would be higher as a result. Part of the accusation was that the students were kicked out of school, thereby, increasing the dropout numbers and rate in hopes of attaining higher test scores. Without notice, the school board member made a public announcement during a school board meeting about the accusation instead of presenting the information to the superintendent's office for investigation, comment, and denial -- how ridiculous an accusation it was. The announcement generated a lot of interest by the local and national media, although the accusation had no merit in fact -- did not happen. Yet, what unfortunately followed were media reports, magazine articles and internet stories, and blogs being written about the situation, treating the accusation as fact, and there was nothing truthful about it. The former employee started the rumor because he was upset about an adverse personnel action taken against him several years before, and he wanted to embarrass the administration by making such a baseless claim. We reminded ourselves of the concept: "Let it go!" Move on to the next issue. We knew to keep the faith in things hoped for even though the evidence was not yet seen that the truth would eventually prevail.

School boards across America hold "closed" or "executive sessions" to discuss personnel matters, legal and contract issues behind closed doors outside of the regular public meeting sessions. We were delighted among school board members and the administration to reduce the time spent in those sessions from an average of two to three hours per meeting to ten to fifteen minutes and no longer than thirty minutes, except in unusual and complicated circumstances. This change was the result of planning together on how to improve the situation and through becoming more focused on which items were administrative and which were about governance and distinguishing which should or should not require school board attention.

The employee association operated like a formal union, including enjoying having in place the largest political action committee in the state of Alabama. The association representatives would sit in the gallery during meetings by the state legislature and point toward the face (eyes) to ask the legislators to vote yes and toward the face (nose) for a vote of no. Such maneuvering was especially important on matters that concerned association members. During my tenure, the state had rules in place, for example, that precluded a school principal from deciding to transfer a campus school teacher from one grade level or subject to another to teach, even if the clear rationale was to ensure the classes were balanced, and the teacher assignment or transfer was needed in one class level or subject instead of another. If the teacher objected to the assignment change, he or she would not have to report to the new class until all appeals had been exhausted. The state appeals committee chairman was the state leader of the association. Teachers sometimes sat in the lounge or outside on the porch during the school days of the appeal period instead of reporting to the class of the new assignment. Nonetheless, it was what it was. We dealt with and maintained the attitude: "Let it go!" Move on to the next issue. We knew to keep the faith – in things hoped for and the evidence of things not yet seen. We found a way to keep the budget balanced and teach the children with the personnel available.

I thought it important to join the employee association for stability and benefits and to enjoy swift access to communiques which were distributed among the members. In one scenario the association members decided to hold an illegal teacher "strike" to protest my new superintendent contract, which required in the contract, among other things, a unanimous vote for non-renewal of the superintendent. The school board and I had taken some strong personnel actions, including termination of contracts for poor performers. The strong job actions, plus training, made a big difference in academic achievement and school district operations.

During the so-called teachers' association "strike" (illegal in Alabama) all schools and centers remained open, but the association thought it would be advantageous for membership recruitment to "stand up" to the superintendent and school board, especially considering the strong job actions which had taken place. I made several public comments in expressing concerns about the association's tactics. One of the leaders in the association advised the superintendent against making such public statements, thereby, allowing the focus to be mainly on myself as opposed to the personnel actions that had spawned the situation in the beginning. Frankly, I was so moved by the teachers' standing up for the association "team" that I had thoughts of joining in with them during their protests -- not a good idea, as I was the decision maker at the time and not really welcomed to join in with them in protesting. The situation was quickly calmed by an action agreed upon by the superintendent and the school board to rescind the original agreement and rework the contract with modified language; albeit, we also actually increased the salary and benefits of the superintendent in the process. All was well with employees and the superintendent, as we all had an opportunity to express our viewpoints. Time for news flash in thinking how best to focus. "Let it go!" Move on to the next issue. We kept the faith.

Just think about it. You would think that everyone would want a new school in their neighborhood, right? Wrong. Not so in several neighborhoods across America and beyond, including the Avondale community, where some community members protested upon learning of the plans to build a new school. Their protest was about what they termed as historical significance of the original school building and that many who remained in the neighborhood either attended the school, or their relatives before them had attended school there. So, what to do? The administration decided to hold public hearings to listen to those whose families lived there at the time or had lived there before, and we listened to the parents whose children were bused to the school from other parts of town -- most students were bused to the school. Eventually, we came to a point of a compromise agreement in which the front façade of the building would be renovated and nicely maintained and manicured to look like a renewal of the original building, and the contractors would build the parts of the new school structure behind the front façade. So, the children would enjoy a new building with a front of the building that looked like the original structure. All was well and time to move on the next issue. "Let it Go!"

We had some remarkably interesting situations to deal with, occasionally, when public officials were able to direct where government funds would go -- commonly known as "pork" funds. This was a fairly common practice in the state of Alabama, with the most senior legislative officials having earned the opportunity to direct the most resources for special projects which they supported. Regrettably, there were times when the administration was challenged to spend the money inappropriately on special projects that would look like children may benefit, but in reality the benefit would be more for other purposes or people, including relatives of the public officials. For example, the legislator would attempt to write in the project description specifications which would enable only family members to benefit from the program.

We said no in those circumstances at any point where things became questionable. Such positions did not sit well at times with the public officials, but our decisions protected them and our school district and administrators who had a role to play in the budget and finance program. We were extremely strict, even to the point of the superintendent avoiding joining meetings with vendors outside of the regular purchasing procedures, policies, and regulations. It did not matter who the vendor knew, or which public official pushed for such meetings. Some of the time the situations were about huge sums of money, for example, United States Government E-rate or schools and libraries technology enhancement funds, where there were very strict guidelines in place for the distribution and spending of the funds. At one time prior to the year 2000, the Birmingham district earned the highest award, per-capita in the nation. Our program was so effective in design and management that we were recognized with a Smithsonian Award in Washington, D. C. for innovation in technology: telephone placed in each regular classroom; each teacher being issued a laptop computer for use in instruction and planning; a computer lab in place in each regular classroom; all school buildings wired for internet access during one summer; and, a computer lab in each school library. We were smart and strong-willed about doing the "right thing" in the spending of the public's money, regardless of who may have suggested otherwise. We practiced "Let it go!" Time for sure to forget it and move on to the next issue.

After leaving the school district, certain members of the school board chose to criticize me and other staff unfairly about how the finance program was managed. At one point I was placed in the position of having to hire an attorney and travel back to Birmingham and hold a news conference to state the facts of my work and tenure and publicly announce my intentions to file a legal suit if my name were used in vain again. There were no more such problems and misstatements or references to the situation following that news conference.

The test scores were so low upon my arrival as superintendent that as many as one-third of the schools rated in the lowest category -- "alert" (low performance) status – in the entire state of Alabama were located in Birmingham, literally, 31 of the 91 in the state. The employees and I moved swiftly to put the conditions in place for turnaround, including making upgrades to our English-Language Arts-Reading curriculum and implementation and mathematics instruction and improving instruction in all other curriculum disciplines. We also put in place accountability standards and followed up with monitoring instruction and supporting school administrators for making the difficult decisions in personnel management. It was unfortunate but despite the "push back" by the employee association, we made the decision to terminate several teachers (and other instructional personnel) by the end of the first year of my work as education leader in Birmingham. We were able to raise test scores at such a swift pace that the education officials at the state level -- Alabama Department of Education led by the State Superintendent of Education, ordered an investigation to determine whether the test scores were legitimate. I thought such action was outrageous but following the investigation, we were cleared of any improper management of the testing program, and the students' scores were declared as legitimate. I can recall receiving a call directly from the State Superintendent in which he reported that no school was on the low performing list for that year— "not one". He and I celebrated during the telephone call, and we quickly made a public announcement about the success story of our dramatic improvement. Yet, still we "Let it go!" Move on to the next issue.

No one is perfect, and even when you believe you have done the best job you can, mistakes can still occur. Such was the case during the first few weeks on the job as education leader in Birmingham, upon presenting to the school board the upgraded administrative organization chart. The staff who assisted in making the chart made a mistake on the last name of one of the school board members on the chart, plugging in the chart with the last name of a popular television personality instead of the school board member's proper last name. The name was close, but close was not good enough. The mistake resulted in some humor at the first observation of the problem by the other school board members, but the humor was not enjoyed by the member whose name was misspelled. We immediately made the correction and learned again the lesson of checking and double checking your work before sharing publicly. We then "Let it go!" Move on to the next issue. We kept the faith.

In school systems, the privilege of serving as the school board president is especially important. It is so important because the person serving in that role serves as the chairperson of school board meetings, determines which items are placed on the meeting agenda for consideration and when, and they serve as the school board representative for programs and media communications. The members will engage in trade-offs and exchanges of favors as part of the bargaining conversations on which member is selected to become the school board president. School board members will sometimes engage in scenarios involving contract management. For example, there was the occasion where the City of Birmingham was poised to provide resources in the form of millions of dollars for construction and renovations of schools through use of interest rates, or savings, from the sale of water to city residents and neighboring city residents. The City of Birmingham was the source of water for several of the surrounding smaller cities. Over $230 million dollars were promised to the school district, which would be combined with resources from the state, totaling over $300 million dollars for our capital improvement program. The city council and mayor had agreed to have the mayor name the program manager, but some of the school board members did not agree, instead wishing that they could name the manager. To receive the funds, the school board had to vote to accept the money.

The school board delayed conducting a meeting for such approval, even postponing a regularly scheduled meeting due to not having a quorum. At that time, the school board was comprised of five members, so three members were required to be in attendance to make a quorum. Two of the members reported they had domestic issues that would prevent their attendance, and another member said that he was too ill to attend. Regrettably, the two who had reported domestic challenges had promised the third member that if he would not attend the meeting, the school board would vote him in as the next president of the school board, a promise that apparently they had no intention of keeping.

During the night following the meeting cancellation, which was during the month of April 1998, the city experienced a very serious tornado which tore into the city with ferocious winds and caused extensive damage to school buildings (including those under construction) and loss of many lives. I met with one of the board members who had missed the board meeting the following morning after the storm at one of the school sites which was damaged. He was extremely interested in the school construction program. I informed him that I had heard about those members who had promised to make him the president and had learned that they had apparently done so only to block the acceptance of the money promised by the city. They had preferences on which companies would be selected for work in the construction program, including program manager. I was able along with two other school board members (who were in agreement with the proposal and program) and attorneys to convince the member to agree to attend an emergency meeting that same day to approve the acceptance of the funds from the City of Birmingham. We would not allow that school board member out of our sight until the meeting. The school board met with only the three members at 1:00 p.m., and the other two again decided not to participate in the meeting.

The meeting lasted only a couple of minutes, with the school board approving the acceptance of the resources offered by the City of Birmingham, including the part about selection of the program manager. Following the meeting, however, within a few days, the person who had served as the school board president announced his retirement from serving on the school board, and those members who had not attended either the regular meeting or the emergency meeting were selected as the president and vice-president of the school board – Uh oh! Sure enough immediately following their selection as officers and the replacement of the school board president with a person who started off playing the role of an antagonist, the two officers called a meeting with me and criticized heavily the role I had played in securing funds for school construction. Go figure. Politics of Education in "real time" and, as too often happens, the emphasis was on personal concerns rather than on positively impacting children. As education leaders we could have stayed "stuck" on what happened and lost our focus, but what we did was continue in our practice to "Let it go!" Move on to the next issue. We were faithful – in things hoped for but evidence yet not seen. We were successful in implementing the capital improvement project for building new schools and renovating others and placing much needed technology in the schools.

Once the mayor selected the company which he preferred to become the program manager, controversy ensued, partly due to their prior work experiences in comparison to the type of work they would be doing with program/project management and the huge amount of money they wanted to charge for the work (partner among two companies). The gap was wide. The school district administration offered a contract with specifications on what work would be completed by the vendor and what work would be completed by the school district employees. The vendor asked for more work and pay at millions of dollars above the one million dollars which we thought would be appropriate -- $9 million they wanted versus the $1 million we offered. On top of the disagreement about the contract, representatives of the media publicly questioned the qualifications of the program manager vendor selected.

The company representatives appealed to the members of the city council and mayor, expressing they thought they had an agreement with city officials for a higher price for the work they had anticipated completing. Following a meeting with the mayor and some city council members one Saturday morning which included members who typically got along in public plus those who did not, I determined that the impasse was too great. By Monday, I had made the determination that I would direct staff to terminate the existing contract we had offered, thereby not to offer a penny more than the portion of the original one million dollars which had been spent on program management. I contacted the mayor and city council president to explain my decision and contacted the vendor as well as distributed a media release announcing to the public the decision that had been made. I was troubled on many levels about the situation prior to the decision, including concerns about the company lobbying public officials for more work and money than was offered and whether there had been promises made to public officials outside of the regular procurement procedure. This was another example of the need to do the right things for the right reasons. It was time to move on regardless of which people did not agree, maintaining our focus on what was best for the children, so what did we do? "Let it go!" Move on to the next issue.

I was honored to enjoy the opportunities and pleasures of visiting the White House in Washington, D. C. several times, including a couple of very special visits I enjoyed upon receiving invitations by the President of The United States in the year 2001, in preparation for the approval of the "No Child Left Behind" (NCLB) legislation and White House Summit on Education. The education legislation meeting included one other public schools' superintendent, state superintendents and commissioners, and governors from around the country. We met in a conference room adjacent to the Oval Office -- about 20 in attendance. President George W. Bush led the meeting on the proposed NCLB legislation and afterwards guided the group on a tour of the Oval Office. Following the meeting and tour, President Bush held a news conference on the outside lawn prior to getting on a helicopter for travel to his next event. The President said that he thought this strategy of such media coverage would have the effect of pressuring the Congress to act sooner than they might otherwise. The attendees were led to an area outside the White House for an additional news conference with representatives of the attendees' local news organizations and national media to speak about and encourage Congress to proceed in passing the education legislation.

In another meeting at the White House, the Summit on Education, educators from several school systems focused primarily on literacy. A reception followed the literacy summit meeting and included several dignitaries, including President George W. Bush and his wife, Mrs. Laura Bush, Vice-President Dick Cheney and his wife, Dr. Lynne Cheney, Secretary of Education, Dr. Rod Paige, and others. I enjoyed the program but admittedly experienced somewhat of an embarrassing glitch with the technology-typewriter style pager device that went off in my suit coat pocket, literally, as President and Mrs. Bush were marching into the reception room. I did not know how to disarm it, as it was brand new and would not turn off automatically. I motioned to the secret service personnel nearby for permission to reach into my pocket to turn the pager off, and punched buttons until it finally was turned off. I was quickly reminded "Let it go!" Move on and focus on the President's message. The honor of my being invited was the result of having served in Houston as the Executive Deputy Superintendent during the time that Dr. Paige served as the superintendent.

* * *

DeKalb County, Georgia – Superintendent. Became a consultant and afterwards assumed the job as superintendent in Port Arthur, Texas. 100,000 Students.

Throughout my career I have been passionate about and outspoken for ensuring that students have equitable learning opportunities, including access to the "top" curriculum offered in each school and school district. In serving as superintendent in DeKalb County, one of the immediate steps I took was to direct that all departments, programs, and personnel be audited to determine whether resources were being distributed and spent fairly, equitably and for the best results in student learning. The audit showed that the school district had spent more money than they had brought in for four of the previous years prior to my arrival. We were facing difficult challenges in making "ends meet" due to low reserves and barely enough money to make payroll. I ordered an immediate halt to new hiring and made the decision to shift more than 20 central office employees to campus level administrative vacancies -- not happy "campers" -- but otherwise we would have been in more trouble financially than we could bear. We also were forced to reduce spending by over $50 million, as much as $45 million during the first year of my serving as the superintendent and seven million the second year. The reductions in spending came primarily from better decision making in personnel and contract management. In addition to decisions for filling campus vacancies with central office personnel, we made other personnel decisions, such as balancing the teacher-student ratio among schools.

The audit revealed that schools were not staffed properly. For example, in one school with a lower enrollment than a neighboring high school, there were as many as 17 more teachers. We made the determination to shift personnel at the winter break for balance and to avoid hiring additional personnel, thereby, more unhappy "campers". The audit also revealed that in some middle schools they were offering courses like algebra and foreign languages for high school credit, while at other middle schools they were not offering such high-level courses. The battle was worth it to ensure equity in such course offerings across the school district. Part of the battle was exposed through public meetings by parents of some of the economically privileged children who had for years enjoyed completing higher level curriculum courses than their peers in other neighborhoods. Those parents went so far as to say loudly in a public school board meeting that we should not burden those children in the not so financially privileged neighborhoods to take courses like high school algebra in middle school because the children would not be as well prepared and would become discouraged. Some of them admitted, however, that what they were really worried about was the prospect that their children would not be as able to get ahead in high school if the "playing field' were leveled by all children being offered the same coursework. The resolution agreed upon by the school board, administration and school leaders was to offer the same high-level curriculum offerings at all middle schools, effective immediately. We worked it out on behalf of the interest of all the children.

When faced with an investigation into school board conduct and other issues by the Southern Association of Colleges and Schools/Council on Accreditation and School Improvement (SACS/CASI) organization, several other administrators and I told the truth and would do so again. The SACS/CASI organization is an international accreditation agency, based in the state of Georgia. In responding to specific questions on whether the school board had conducted itself in accordance with the rules and policies on governance, I responded with truthful answers. For example, one question was whether the school board had taken steps to delay or block efforts by the administration to provide equitable opportunities to all children in academic course offerings, such as middle school algebra for high school credit. Following the submission of the responses to SACS/CASI, the school board held "private" meetings with attorneys representing the school district and SACS/CASI. School board members did not invite me or others in the administration to attend those meetings. This was obviously a reflection of their disdain for the answers the administration had submitted, which they thought were not favorable to them as a school board or personally. I knew then and continue to believe that the best approach was to tell the truth and "Let it go!" Move on to the next issue, in thinking that "all you can do is all you can do". Always tell the truth on behalf of the children and always do right by them, even while knowing or believing that the consequences may not end up being favorable to you, professionally or personally. I kept the faith – in things hoped for and the evidence of things not yet seen.

Speaking on governance and how things can move in the wrong direction, there is no one who wishes to be accused of something based on the "rumor mill" when the information is not true. Such was the case of an emergency called school board meeting during which the school board grilled me on what they explained was a rumor brought to them by a school administrator(s) who had spawned the notion that I had given directions to principals that were inconsistent with what the school board had wanted with respect to the "dress for success" program. The program implementation had gone extremely well, with complaints from only a few parents who complained publicly -- albeit, loudly among the few, gaining the attention and concern of some members of the school board. In fact, I was so confident and open about the dress code implementation that I discussed the dress code initiative on a nationally televised CNN program, hosted by Fredricka Whitfield that included a parent opposed to the concept. The dress code directions were clear and distributed in writing, but apparently one or more principals gave the impression to school board members, directly or indirectly, that behind the scenes the administration had added stricter guidelines that were contrary to the wishes of the school board. The meeting was not a comfortable experience as the thrust of it was an accusation that was not based on reality or actual actions that had been taken by me or others in the administration. Another good time to "Let it go!" Move on the next issue, which I was glad to do.

Continuing with the Politics of Education as related to school governance and oversight by school board members, can you believe that a school board member would contact the superintendent to express outrage about some things she had heard from parents living in her district/neighborhood that a person parents did not like or respect was being considered for promotion, and, if so, they asked the board member to make sure that person was not selected for a promotion to supervise schools in their neighborhood? Yes, it did happen and, of course, it did not affect consideration of a professional's selection for a job. What do you do in such situations, where you are balancing the need to do what is right with the need to be cooperative with your school board member? The answer is you do the right thing, 100 percent of the time -- do what is right by and supportive of the children and employees, and then "Let it go!" Move on to the next issue.

One of the more amazing revelations I encountered as an education leader was to be made aware of payments to a local news reporter by non-supportive detractors to publish negative and inaccurate stories that were intended to harm and disrupt the reform agenda of the school district administration. For example, "fake news" stories were published stating that the administration was secretly designing a plan to close as many as 16 neighborhood schools, mostly elementary schools. Nothing in the story was based on reality. The story resulted in confusion and alarm among many in the community, and we had to work hard to correct the inaccuracies. We learned a lot about how far people will go to distract education leaders away from focusing on helping the children learn and teachers teach. Yet, in leadership it is important to remember that regardless of whether their intentions are honorable or not so honorable, you always must keep your "guard up" and believe that someone is always watching and may or may not support the reform agenda. So, in leadership you should carry yourself as you would if you were performing in front of the public on television or on a public program stage. Not easy following such odd revelations, but we had to "Let it go!" Move on to the next issue. And we noted, it is important to keep the faith – in things hoped for but evidence not seen.

A DeKalb School Board member openly complained to the superintendent about her not liking and not respecting key administrative personnel. She even commented, "Better to let the district crash and burn than to support and keep them employed". She also complained about the publication of a book which one of the administrators had written and had widely shared information about the book with employees. It was not easy to operate with knowledge of such an attitude. Yet, we education leaders knew our best option was to do the right thing and "Let it go!" Move on to the next issue. As education leaders it is important to do the "right thing" all the time.

As many as three school board members asked me to attend a luncheon for the purpose of discussing the creation of an administrative position as a reward for the campaign manager of one of the school board members. The person was not qualified for such a position, and the idea was rejected outright. The administrative response, albeit correct, resulted in dissention between the superintendent and the members who were advocates for the person being employed in the school district. It was clear again that the best approach was to do the right thing and "Let it go!" Move on to the next issue and "keep the faith" that by doing the "right" thing that things will work out fine.

It is amazing the kinds of things that public officials will trade off to gain advantage for issues that they support. One area in school board politics that sometimes is the focus of the trade-off is about which person will become the school board president. I have observed this reality in a couple of school systems, Birmingham, Alabama, as described earlier, and DeKalb County, Georgia. In Birmingham the offer was for a school board member to be selected as the board president if he would miss an important meeting regarding the school facilities program where the school board was asked to vote to accept $230 million dollars from the City of Birmingham. In DeKalb County, Georgia a deal was made by some members that would affect the contract of the superintendent around the issue of who would become the next school board president. Serious "stuff" and incredibly sad, but real, nonetheless. Following the adverse contractual action taken by the school board the best attitude that would follow was "Let it go!" Move on to the next issue. We kept the faith in those things hoped for but evidence not seen.

In this school district there were routine occasions where those in governance disregarded their officially designated roles and crossed into the "lanes" of the administration when it had to do with personnel and contract management. For example, they would dictate which personnel to hire and not to hire or keep and which contracts to issue or cancel, including in some instances concerned with members of their families. The administration stood strong and steady and avoided the predictable political pressure in terms of job security. Yet, we realized that for each situation there would be the potential of fallout and disgruntlement by those who did not get their way. We worked consistently based upon the concept: "Let it go!" Do the right thing, and move on to the next issue.

* * *

Port Arthur Independent School District, Texas – Superintendent. 9,100 Students.

The school district was managed under State of Texas control for 18 months prior to my assuming the position of superintendent due to various issues such as governance, test scores, facilities management, and budget concerns. It was important to analyze the situation and move swiftly in building positive relationships among all concerned and making decisions about why things were what they were, what to do - how, how much, when and where - and to determine how to measure progress, successes, and related outcomes. Once I decided to take the job, I worked hard each day to do the right thing in support of the children. Under my leadership and cooperation of the school board, we were able to end the state management within one month from the start of my tenure as education leader. I tried always to align myself with those who agreed to be part of the "team of reformers," with the understanding that not everyone would belong to such a reform minded group, and not everyone would be on our side when engaged in a major turnaround effort. We were successful within and across all areas of leadership and reform, including: (a) raising student test scores by double digits across all grade levels in the school district; (b) building new schools -- including Memorial High School, for which construction was delayed for several years before my tenure due to a disagreement about the school site; (c) building other new schools and completing major renovations for all other schools, not new; (d) passing a huge school bond election for capital improvements; (e) balancing the budget and increasing emergency reserves; (f) increasing parental engagement; (g) reducing the dropout rate and increasing the attendance rate of students and staff; and (h) reducing incidents of discipline infractions, and other general improvements and successes. Not surprisingly, there was push-back by those who did not associate themselves with the "team of reformers" or for whom they were affected by personnel or other changes with which they disagreed. Some of them reacted very unprofessionally and attempted to stop the reform changes by failing to work effectively or spreading insults and various types of false accusations with the clear intention of blocking reforms through attacks on leadership and other reformers.

One of the reminders that resulted from the work among such resistance was to be careful in leadership never to get too comfortable with others in the work environment and to always remain focused on the mission -- on what you intend to accomplish. I was reminded to be clear on the purpose of reform efforts and desired outcomes and not to be afraid to speak up with clarity when needed. Things are not always fair in leadership or in life. As education leader it was truly clear that the best option for moving forward was to "Let it go!" Move on to the next issue. Focus on taking care of the children and their interests.

Once on the job, the administration decided that we had to make personnel changes, especially in administration. We made over 20 administrative changes, including central office and school campus leadership shifts. Most of the changes were well received by the school board, employees, and community. There were some who were directly affected by the changes who protested, mostly silently or among peers. There were others who showed they were disgruntled more openly, including focus upon who was in the job of principal at a few of the schools. Some of the types of challenges we faced were the result of familiarity of those who had served as principal for an extended time – but schools not successful under their leadership. Questions were also raised by detractors about the key roles that some of the women would play, as women usually had not assumed such positions in the past -- such as lead principal of the high school. It was a sad reality but true that we faced opposition about selecting women for certain leadership positions because of their gender. We made the decisions on what we determined were in the best interest of the children and then we decided to "Let it go!" Move on to the next issue. We were proud to name women on two separate occasions to serve as the high school principal, and both were successful in providing leadership. We were also proud to name women for other key leadership roles in the school district, such as chief financial officer/assistant superintendent for business and finance -- also successful in leadership.

The current high school building is located a few miles from the original high school building and was built using funds primarily from the bond program which was passed several years prior to the final decision on the current site. From the time that the first bond had passed which occurred prior to my tenure, inflation increased the cost by millions of dollars. We were faced with the need to pass a second multi-million-dollar bond issue to be able to complete the entire project, as designed. Part of the argument which caused the delay had to do with those who thought it better to rebuild the school on the original lot, which was far smaller in acreage than the new (current) site. The other major issue was that some representatives of the neighborhood where the school now sits were against placing the school in their neighborhood. It appeared to be a matter of race and class and fear of the unknown, in thinking that the students who would attend the school would not act appropriately. Finally, it was a matter of courage for making the right decision with the children's best interest in mind. I declared soon upon my arrival during a meeting of the ninth graders that they would graduate from the new high school building; and they did just that! A few onlookers criticized me for making such an announcement. I explained to them that what I was operating under was a full understanding of the facts on acreage and available resources and what was in the best interest of the children. We marched forward and got the school built, and then we "Let it go!" Move on to the next issue.

In education leadership, governance is a huge factor in determining success, including the roles and responsibilities and relationships of the school board and superintendent; positive is always better. For most school boards in Texas, there are seven school board members. Larger systems may have as many as nine school board members. In either case, a one-member change can make the difference whether the superintendent-school board relationship is positive and productive or not. In the case of Port Arthur, most of the original seven school board members who were in place when I was hired were not in place when I departed the school district. In fact, there were only two of the original seven serving at the end of my tenure in 2013. So, the school board composition included different members as I left the school district, including some who brought to the table viewpoints which were significantly different regarding the reform agenda in place. They also differed on what constitutes the appropriate role of the "governors" and administration with respect to micromanagement. This factor in Port Arthur and, indeed, across the nation is no small matter. Yet, it is helpful for those in education leadership to remember the concept, when the time comes "Let it go!" Move on to the next issue or place. I have kept the faith – in things hoped for and the evidence of things not yet seen.

* * *

General Comments on Circumstances in Politics of Education

In participating in interviews for the job of superintendent, school districts used different formats and methods for selection. In some cases, the search consultant conducted the initial interviews for paring down the pool of candidates prior to interviews to be conducted by the school boards. In other cases, the school boards themselves determined which candidates to interview. The interviews were either private and conducted behind closed doors, or in other cases the interviews were held in public and shown on live television with print media representatives present. I was fortunate to enjoy the experience in several different settings and scenarios, for example, in Toledo, Ohio, where the interview was televised. At the time I was the deputy superintendent for educational programs in Cleveland, Ohio, and was recruited by a search consultant to consider the job. The interview appeared to go well. However, I found some of the questions raised by school board members to be quite odd. One question raised pertained to the Cleveland superintendent, my direct supervisor, asking whether I was currently working for a person who would "aim, aim, aim" and fail to decide in difficult circumstances. The reception which followed the interview and included all finalists was also odd, as the city mayor attended and made disparaging comments about each candidate during television interviews, saying that he did not believe either candidate was qualified for the job. It was not kind and not professional. During another televised interview in Memphis, Tennessee for the job of superintendent, the school board members appeared to engage in a battle among themselves by asking questions they thought may favor a certain candidate, only to be interrupted by another school board member who appeared to be favorable to me who would assist in answering the questions. Admittedly, I was reluctant to interview for either job. And I seriously doubted I would accept a job offer from either place, even prior to the interviews. I was not selected for the Ohio job and declined to complete the process in Tennessee, explaining to the search consultant that I did not believe the job would be a good "fit" and I thought the timing was not good.

One of the most interesting experiences along the path of job searching was when I was recruited to travel from Cleveland, Ohio, to Oakland, California, for an interview for the job of superintendent. During the night following the interview, my wife, Carolyn, and I found ourselves experiencing an earthquake that shook the hotel room early in the morning where we were staying. It was an alarming experience, for sure, although we were not certain at the time about what was going on. Not being from California and having no earthquake experience we thought someone was breaking into our hotel room. Next morning as we were checking out of the hotel, we found out what had happened. I also experienced alarm and fear in traveling from Austin, Texas, to Cleveland, Ohio, by flight during the time of a blizzard that had blanketed the entire northeast portion of the United States, including Cleveland. The flight which would ordinarily entail three hours took me seventeen hours, including a layover stop in Chicago, Illinois. I can recall the pilot upon leaving O'Hare International Airport saying that he thought we could complete the flight successfully. About three-quarters of the way into the flight, the pilot announced that the storm had worsened in Cleveland but it would be better to try to land rather than return back to Chicago, due to considerations of gasoline and other matters. He announced that he was going to try to land the plane in the middle of the blizzard conditions at the airport, where the snow was falling so fast the airport's ground crew was not able to create the safe space that would ordinarily be required for such a landing to occur. As the plane connected to the tarmac of the airport, the passengers in unison applauded in a joyful response that we had landed safely. The next challenge that followed was in securing transportation from the airport to the hotel, as the roads were overlaid by snow and challenging for automobiles to navigate safely. I was able to grab a taxi for safe transportation to the hotel, and I made it to the interview on time and got the job!

While I am proud of being selected for the jobs that I have held and that I served proudly as deputy superintendent and superintendent, I was also honored to be selected as finalist for jobs for which I was not selected. One such special place where I was honored to be selected as a finalist for the job of superintendent was my home city, Austin, Texas. This was a national search, and few candidates were selected as finalists. While I was disappointed about not being selected, I was reassured that the person chosen had an impressive background and a record of success as superintendent. I was also proud of and thankful for being named as a finalist (runner up) for the job of superintendent of the Round Rock Independent School District, a neighboring school district of Austin, although another candidate was selected for the job. This situation was another national search, and the person selected had worked in the Round Rock system previously.

I ran for a position on the school board in Port Arthur following the completion of my tenure as superintendent. I offered to serve as I believed that I had a lot to offer. While I did not win a seat on the school board, I enjoyed the experience of meeting with the community and faculty and staff and youth during the election process—lost by 43 votes. No problem and the idea for entering the race was to offer support to the children in a new role. I remained busy in helping in other ways, such as raising funds for senior high school scholarships through community organizations of which I am affiliated – Rotary Club of Port Arthur and 100 Black Men of Greater Beaumont. I did not spend even a minute pouting or complaining. "Let it go!" Move on to the next issue.

One of the difficult circumstances that school districts and administrative personnel sometimes experience following the exit of a superintendent is unfriendly, unprofessional, and unfair treatment for those employees who remain. Those situations may also include dismantling of programs put in place by the superintendent before leaving. It is wise for superintendents and members of the executive team to include in their contracts or gain a clear understanding up front on what happens with executive and campus level leadership once the superintendent exits the job. The better approach for the incoming and departing superintendent and school boards is always to operate with integrity, fairness in terms of treatment of personnel and laser focus on what is best for the children.

In the politics of education, it is important to consider demands on the time of the superintendent, campus principals, executive and instructional staff, with special emphasis on time on task. Such demands on time include meetings and programs during and after the regular duty day associated with the school district and community. This issue should not be left to chance and should be handled as part of any strategic planning process. This call for action is not limited to administrative personnel, as each employee and the children deserve to have the time it takes for success in each position. Educators should spend their time on the priorities that will best serve the children and not allow themselves to be distracted in efforts to try to make everyone happy. Also, watch out for those employees who may show up every day for the job but are not competent in achieving expected results. It is important to balance the time on critical tasks with those of otherwise nice but unnecessary time-consuming projects and meetings or realize the maximum results for the children are not likely to be achieved.

Everyone agrees that accountability is important in any business or organization. In education there are huge challenges including, but not limited to, lack of clarity on who is in charge at the school district level and at campuses. There are too often barriers on leadership being able to make decisions or not being able to act due to people with perceived power blocking the way. Consider, for example, a school principal who identifies a teacher who is not performing as expected and believes termination is the best personnel action, following numerous observations, opportunities for staff development, reprimands, and poor student performance. Any such final job action for termination in the states I have worked in takes months if not years and thousands of dollars in legal fees by the school district and agreement by the superintendent, attorney, and school board and winning at the appeal level. If the superintendent and/or majority of the school board do not agree with the campus principal, the termination is delayed or blocked. The system in place is designed to hire the best education leader at each school and school district, but when it is time to demonstrate trust and confidence in such leaders and their decision making, too often it is not there. Therefore, the leaders tend to avoid making the difficult decisions because they believe the time and hassle are not worth it. Of course, due process is important, but even when there is agreement by the school board, superintendent, and campus principal on the need for termination, the process in place takes months and exorbitant legal fees to complete. <u>The time is long overdue for legislative action at the state and federal levels to enable school leaders to hold staff accountable for results in a manner that is less expensive and not so time consuming</u>. If the parents and community truly expect to hold school principals, superintendents, and other instructional personnel accountable for results in student performance, the rules must be established and enforced to become aligned with that expectation.

I was reminded, upon accepting roles as education leader in

problematic situations such as in Birmingham, Alabama, Port Arthur, and Wilmer-Hutchins in Texas and DeKalb County, Georgia, of an important point. That is, in making decisions on personnel actions that the relatives and close friends of those affected by the job actions react and often line up to fight the leader, sometimes on a personal basis, and they never go away -- enemy for the rest of the tenure of the leader. The same holds true in shifts made to the organizational design, selection of vendors for contracts and more. So, what to do, always do the right thing on behalf of the children and let "the chips fall where they may". Keep the "faith" no matter the challenges.

It is often stated that we should hold all children to high standards and expectations. Yet, often the statement refers to some, not all children, and the children of low income and minority race communities are not considered as capable. Whether said directly or not that we hold some children to higher expectations than others, look at policies and procedures in a school district. For example, in multiple school districts I have worked in as education leader, children are discouraged, and rules are in place to block them from taking advanced placement coursework in high school. There is no rule by the College Board organization to restrict students from enrolling in such courses, and some programs, such as the High Schools That Work initiative, encourage each student to complete at least one advanced placement course prior to graduation. We should continue to encourage our youth to prepare well in early years, of course. But we should also encourage all children to take on the challenge of enrolling in higher order thinking courses, such as calculus and other upper level mathematics coursework, physics and more. The question is not whether students are capable of learning but whether we as adults are willing to open the doors of opportunity for all children and ensure that we have in place a high quality, concerned teacher in each classroom.

Educators and parents sometimes make statements such as "All Children Can Learn" and "All Children Deserve the Opportunity to Learn" or "All Children Will Learn", but for many individuals these are only words, not beliefs. In one of the school systems I served as superintendent, I attended an evening parent/community meeting upon invitation by one of the school board members where the topic of discussion was the development of a strategy to control or reduce the number and percentage of federal program "Title 1" students (as defined by government free-reduced lunch eligibility or low-income) and those children who lived in apartments. Those responsible for leading the meeting had prepared reports which reflected the percentage of children mapped in accordance to the neighborhoods they lived in and aligned with the "Title 1" population of children. Statements were made including ideas such as "We have served our share of these children." "They are responsible for bringing our test scores down". Interestingly, my family lived in an apartment at the time of the meeting, and one of our daughters attended the specific school in which the meeting was held. Every child is important and deserves to be treated with respect and dignity and as a precious human being whom we adults should be proud to serve.

Among those experiences of great pleasure, at or near the top of the list was the opportunity to meet with students, grades six through twelve in the sessions that we named Student Advisory Council, or Committee depending upon the school district. The meetings were scheduled for five – six times during the school year, and the students were selected by the campus leadership according to established criteria, considering such factors as: diversity by gender and race; student performance -- high level achievers and reluctant learners; grade level representation -- sixth through twelfth, noting that once selected for the committee, students would continue as they moved upward in grade level assignments. New sixth graders were added each year as seniors departed. The agenda was clear and practical, that is: What is going on in your school that is "right", and what is going on that is not so "right"? If not "right" make suggestions for corrections or improvements. The program was implemented as I served as superintendent in Birmingham, Alabama, DeKalb County, Georgia and Port Arthur, Texas.

We typically began and ended each meeting with the members of the senior class giving advice to the underclassmen and making general comments. There was no exception, regardless of the school district, in terms of the high quality of comments from students at all levels. We never ever had to correct students about their behavior or remind them to listen to others as they spoke. We found that when children are treated with respect and dignity, they perform as expected.

Students always dressed nicely and raised important, relevant topics for discussion regarding the curriculum, quality of leadership and teaching, instruction, and level of concern demonstrated by faculty and staff. Generally, the discussions were about whether the students' learning experiences were productive and high level and, if not, about what the problems were and suggestions for improvement.

We kept notes and shared those notes across the school system following each meeting, and we encouraged the students to speak candidly. We informed all faculty and staff that the students would be treated with respect upon returning to their campuses and not criticized for giving their opinions. Students were provided with contact information directly associated with the office of the superintendent to enable them to reach the superintendent in times of questions or concerns and to report any incidents of pressure being applied before or following meetings about what they said or planned to say. The last part of these meetings almost always resulted in tearjerker situations, as senior level students shared which universities they would attend and major fields they would study. They also gave closing remarks to encourage the underclassmen, sometimes by sharing favorite poems and quotes and at other times advising the younger students to work hard and focus on excellence in achievement. In a couple of the school districts on occasion we sang songs at the start of the meetings to ensure a joyful mood and gain engagement by all. For example, we sang the tune that follows:

> *The Jesus in me loves the Jesus in you.*
> *The Jesus in me loves the Jesus in you.*
> *So easy, so easy, so easy, easy to love.*
> *The joy in me loves the joy in you,*
> *The joy in me loves the joy in you,*
> *So easy, so easy, so easy,*
> *Easy to love.*
> *(Author unknown).*

We borrowed the song from The St. Luke Community United Methodist Church in Dallas where the choir sang it when the Reverend,

Dr. Zan Holmes was senior pastor. We substituted the word "good" for Jesus to avoid challenges with legal issues on religion in schools. The song is widely shared in many churches across the globe. We were so confident in how these meetings would go that we routinely invited the media to attend.

Suggestions on governance framework which could result in the following outcomes: higher student achievement; more equitable and adequate distribution of resources; lower level of local political influence; improved accountability among employees; and smoother alignment between state expectations and accomplishments on a local level. The first suggestion is to place local superintendents and school districts under management of the state through regional service centers and have the school boards serve in an advisory capacity. In such a framework, the state commissioner or state superintendent would employ "super" superintendents at the regional level who would report directly to the state, and local superintendents would report to those "super" superintendents. On selection and evaluation, that process would be managed through the regional "super" superintendent, in coordination with the state commissioner or state superintendent and advisory school board. Again, the school board would serve in an advisory capacity and have a role to play in providing input on the selection, performance, and evaluation of the superintendent and local system priorities. I also suggest that as a minimum requirement on qualifications for the state commissioner or state superintendent, the person serving in that role must have enjoyed time in education as a teacher, administrator, or school board member prior to selection.

Chapter Seven

Excellence in Leadership and Travel Highlights

I enjoyed the campus and central office positions where I had a direct role in influencing curriculum and school operations. No doubt, the coaching experiences in San Antonio and Austin, Texas were fun, and we enjoyed success in winning games and the rewards of being part of the team or "extended family" as can often be the case in athletics. I was also fortunate that in each case of serving as central office administrator, including the roles of deputy superintendent and superintendent, I had the good sense, knowledge and preparation as required to primarily focus attention on supporting the children in the classroom. Period.

As part of the growth, development, and travel exploration experiences, I have enjoyed visiting most states and several Indian reservations in the United States, with special interest in the urban centers and numerous cities and countries across the world. Examples of such travel: Banjul in The Gambia and Accra, Ghana in West Africa; Brussels, Belgium; Amsterdam, Rotterdam and The Hague in The Netherlands; Cologne, Heidelberg and other cities in Germany; Paris and Nice, France; London, England; Luxembourg, Luxembourg; Nassau, in The Bahamas; Nuevo Laredo and Tijuana, Mexico; Windsor and Niagara Falls, Ontario, Canada. I lived in four states in The United States of America: Texas, born, reared and lived most years; Alabama; Georgia, and Ohio.

In visits to each of the countries I visited outside of the United States, I was impressed with and proud of meeting many people of different backgrounds and life experiences. I looked for and found positive things and friendly people in each place. Such visits have been validation of many books and reports I have read and observations I have made that people really are more similar than different. They have needs and desires and preferences, likes and dislikes, objects and people they love and others they do not. They tend to live around and associate with other people who are alike and whose thoughts and actions align with those like themselves. I admire those cities, states, and countries where diversity appears to be a priority and is celebrated and where people live and dine and associate routinely within and across racial and income lines. One of the ways to determine how a place operates is to look at its housing patterns, in terms of integration or segregation by race and class. Another point of interest is to study income patterns within and across the races.

Among other highlights in visiting foreign lands, I was very observant of similarities and differences in human interactions and the environment. For example, in visiting the magnificent castles in London, England and several similar sites in Germany, there were clear contrasts when compared to places with extreme poverty I visited, such as Accra, Ghana and Banjul, The Gambia in West Africa. Yet, no matter which place I visited in each country and state in the United States, I encountered mostly nice, friendly, intelligent, and caring people. Of course, not everyone in West Africa is poor and not everyone in England and Germany is rich or privileged. One memory of note while visiting Banjul was the way store owners covered for each other in managing and assisting customers. It was not unusual to observe an owner of one establishment leave his or her shop in the care of the owner of a nearby shop. It was also routine for residents to share the lunchtime meal in the town square, for example, bowl of soup-like substance where all around would kneel above the large bowl and partake of what was inside, using their hands to scoop up the food and eat. I chose not to participate in that ritual. Each trip overseas was memorable in observing and learning about foreign lands and cultures and in building upon the history lessons that included reference to places that Carolyn and I were able to visit: The Louvre Museum, The Avenue des Champs-Elysees and the Eiffel Tower in Paris, France; The Palace of Versailles in Versailles, France; Buckingham Palace, Kensington Palace and the Tower of London in London, England; University of Oxford in Oxford, England; Stratford-upon-Avon, Warwickshire, England; Anne Frank House in Amsterdam, the Netherlands; The Hague in the Netherlands; Heidelberg and other castles in Germany.

My family and I have enjoyed the pleasure of visiting most states in the United States. I looked at it as a true gift of life to enjoy the opportunities to travel to so many different places and to live in four states: Alabama, Georgia, Ohio, and Texas. We were fortunate to find joy within and across several cities and attractions in each of these states.

Carolyn and I enjoy and support the arts. So much so that we encouraged and provided leadership for the Port Arthur school district and community to support the program the sponsors called "A Classroom Without Walls". For two years this program entailed organizing and sponsoring fine arts trips for the students involved in the fine arts departments of our high school. We traveled with students and chaperones to New York City to enjoy Broadway plays and other tourist and cultural sites of the city. For some of the students, it was the first time flying on an airplane among other first-time exposures. We scheduled dance classes with professional actresses held at a music studio, and we took tours of museums, the Apollo Theatre, The Federal Reserve Bank and NBC studios -- saw Miley Cyrus performing in a practice session for an upcoming Saturday Night Live show. Additionally, we toured key areas of the city, such as the original Macy's store, and attended a National Basketball Association game between the New York Knicks and the Cleveland Cavaliers at Madison Square Garden. We walked through parts of Times Square and dined at famous restaurants such as the Hard Rock Café. On a separate visit to New York City prior to the first student trip, I was inspired by the Broadway production of the Lion King and observed that the audience was not diverse in terms of the youth in attendance. I was convinced that the students in Port Arthur would enjoy such a Broadway play if given the opportunity. Indeed, they enjoyed seeing the Lion King and two other Broadway shows: Memphis and West Side Story. Several years later Carolyn and I were privileged to return and attend two excellent Broadway shows: Hamilton and Ain't Too Proud--The Life and Times of The Temptations -- both outstanding! We also enjoyed numerous other Broadway plays in earlier years in New York, such as Oklahoma!, Cat on a Hot Tin Roof, featuring a host of popular, experienced artists: Terrence Howard, Phylicia Rashad, James Earl Jones, Anika Noni Rose and others. Finally, we have had the pleasure of attending several times the play The Color Purple in multiple venues.

Of course, these opportunities for the youth would not have been possible without the cooperation, planning and support of a team of professionals and chaperones, led by the high school principal, and band director, Trenton Johnson, and other employees, especially, the fine arts supervisor, Marjorie Cole, with the strong support of the school board. Students and their parents were required to assist in the planning and raising of funds and in conducting research on the city's history and programs that we visited. The students conducted research prior to the trip and were required to write reports afterwards, for example, reporting on the financial district and Wall Street and how it operates. We also visited the United Nations, the Empire State Building and took a ferry to a tour of Ellis Island and the Statue of Liberty. No doubt this was a fine learning and growth opportunity for our youth. The arts help to give meaning to life and serve as a major inspiration to our youth and adults. So often the arts are underfunded in the public schools, and youth miss the opportunity to grow and prosper in this arena. The arts are an important factor in our enjoyment of life, as just about every program at church, school, and other venues begin with music or artistic performances -- the top performers typically began training during their youth.

I believed it was important to support the youth for wide exposure to the arts as part of their educational experience. It was such a priority in leadership that I monitored the budget to ensure provision of adequate resources dedicated to the fine arts programs. It was the right approach and morally significant.

I have witnessed and experienced joy and happiness as well as disappointment and other emotions in my work, travel, and life in general. It is noticeably clear that regardless of the place, we all are in search for a higher quality of life, love and happiness. We all deserve it. Unfortunately, it seems that a person does not have to look far to find that no matter how much we all wish and deserve such positive opportunities, there are people around who prefer to distract from the good and seek to harm others. With respect to the types of conduct which may be very harmful to others, included among other unkind emotions and attitudes is discrimination by race and class, denial of opportunities for education, jobs and life status and segregation by neighborhood makeup, economics and otherwise. I am, however, encouraged that things will change for the better over time. I have kept the faith – in things hoped for and the evidence of things not yet seen.

I believe it is better to be humble in style and approach in communication with others. One encounter that I found humbling and still humorous occurred with a student in an elementary classroom that I visited in Birmingham, Alabama, where I served as superintendent. The young student struggled to remember my name. He eventually said that he had it and in front of the entire class loudly yelled out the name of former President Bill Clinton, instead of my name. It really did not matter but brought me back to earth for that day and afterward. I was under the misconception that this student and his classmates were excited because they recognized me as an important person in their midst, but, of course, the most important people in the room were the children. I felt honored that he placed me with a former United States president.

The emphasis in schooling must always be on the children as we educators, parents, and community members work to ensure an environment for success and excellence. Therefore, the focus in our thoughts and actions require devotion and passion toward ensuring meaningful understanding and absolute clarity on the purpose of our childhood preparations and encounters -- emphasis on purpose! That is, thinking based on a champion mentality and purpose which encompasses the team concept, where each member (child) is valued. Each? Yes, each child. We must remember that what is seen or observed is reality. Whenever an organization has people associated with it who fail to or show reluctance to demonstrate understanding, passion, and beliefs in the agreed upon purpose and appreciation of each person, the system breaks down. Team means all are valued, not some treated as valued and others not so valued. I believe that most people are honorable and caring and want to do the right thing. Just as it often takes the leadership of one person to make the difference for positive change, the same holds true for the possibility that one person can destroy and act to block such progress.

MEET
THE
EMERSON STREET FAMILY

91

FAMILY

SPORTS

Professional Life

Chapter Eight

Race, Class and Quality of Life

Everyone deserves and yearns for a high quality of life, as related to many factors: good health of family and self; safety of self and family; a positive family environment; resources available for all basic comforts, needs and preferences; a nice home located in a friendly, safe neighborhood; an automobile or other appropriate transportation; a happy, supportive and satisfying everyday lifestyle; a gratifying job with the potential for advancement and income increases; and adequate reserve funds for emergencies. The reality is that we humans live and operate according to a pattern defined by class -- social status, rank, common attributes, and wealth. The pattern allows for some shifting into or out of a designated status as a person experiences changes in his or her lifestyle or wealth. I have not met a person who strives to become less wealthy. I have also not met a person who wishes to live a lower quality of life.

There are many highlights that could be reported for applause on the positive aspects of history, current conditions, and predictable future of my great country, the United States of America. However, there are other highlights that are not to be applauded, on the "dark side" of our history, current conditions, and, unfortunately, predictable future of the country. Among the worst historical realities to acknowledge are the existence and cruelties of slavery in America for more than 240 years— from 1619 to 1865 (Thirteenth Amendment to the U. S. Constitution).

The nation allowed by law the practice and pattern of enslaving people of African descent, treating them as unwilling and oppressed servants or beasts, totally against their wishes. Beyond 1865 the so-called Jim Crow laws ruled much of the land, where states adopted statutes and ordinances following 1865 to the mid-1970s to openly tolerate and encourage the hatred and atmosphere of superiority and to keep the races physically and otherwise segregated, particularly in the southern parts of the country, under the concept of "separate but equal". In those times of slavery and beyond during the times of Jim Crow, not only were things not equal for all, the oppression persisted, and equality was not the standard which was practiced. The inequalities were evident in public facilities: hotels; service stations; restaurants; law enforcement; education; court systems that allowed the application of biases; theatres that were not widely accessible; restricted voting; and more. Not only was equality not achieved for an awfully long time after 1865, but people not of color were able to enjoy privileges unavailable to those of color, and Jim Crow laws allowed such separation. People of color were left to tolerate such poor living standards and experience more punitive consequences.

I vividly remember some of those regrettable days. For example, during my early years of development, there were separate water fountains and bathrooms for African Americans and Whites at service stations and other environments. I referenced earlier in the text the incident where a neighborhood friend and I went inside a local Austin area pharmacy soda fountain bar area, and I was told to go outside to drink my beverage. The White friend was not given such directions and could enjoy his drink inside; although, he chose to leave with me. I also remember the movie theatres, separating the races from sitting in the same theatres. In downtown Austin in one theatre African Americans could attend the same theatre but were required to sit upstairs while the Whites sat downstairs. Each year while in elementary school, we traveled to hear the local Austin, Texas, area orchestra perform at the convention center, but the children were segregated by race regarding where they would be directed to sit.

The benefits of diversity are wide and often extraordinary as reflective either through coincidental encounters or the result of events which are planned. I thoroughly enjoyed, for example, the undergraduate and graduate university experiences in communicating with fellow students and professors, representing multiple races, cultures, and geographical regions of the nation -- including rural areas of Texas. I also enjoyed the grade school years of communications and events with classmates and neighbors, including basketball teammates and others from diverse backgrounds and circumstances. We laughed at funny jokes and situations and sometimes risks we took in fun, and we frowned and even cried at times of sorrow. Such positive opportunities also presented themselves beyond the grade school and university years in the "world of work". I learned to listen with more heightened attention to country music, as several of the coaches I worked with were dedicated to and enjoyed such music. In turn, they paid more attention to soul music and rock and roll style tunes. I even spent time at social events with other coaches -- beautiful picture of diversity -- where the music played was, primarily, country and western, and all present enjoyed singing and dancing and enjoying life. The pattern was reciprocal as the group also attended social events where the music enjoyed was soul, rhythm and blues, and rock and roll style.

In this nation, we have changed how we govern and operate to a large extent, and yet there remains a long way to go before we can truly declare the victory of a fair, equitable, post racial society. Many of those whose hearts appeared to be opposed to change over the course of our history have opened their hearts and minds to better understand the need to make progress toward a more perfect nation. Indeed, we need a nation which includes models and practices for shaping the environment to become more focused on the common good and equality for all. It will be a better world for all when we routinely show an advent attitude of looking for good in others and treating all with dignity and respect. Also, it is better to show humble tendencies over arrogance and superiority. Throughout history the greatest leaders of government and civil and human rights advocates have consistently demonstrated these positive and progressive attitudes. Such leaders, joined by numerous other ordinary citizens, have shown a visible "air" of humility and concern for helping others and an attitude of pressing for the common good over self-interests. It will take everyone, not just the outstanding leaders and their followers, to enable the nation to make the kind of progress needed to "fill" the "glass" to overflow with the good over the negative. Then and then only will we profoundly move toward the need to replace it with a "taller" glass of good will and high quality of life for all.

There is little question about it, the politics of the nation and the effect on organizations such as businesses, schools and school districts often drive decisions that affect the common good, adversely. Compare and contrast, for example, the national politics and general mood of the nation, comparing the years between 2008 and 2016 and the years which immediately followed. The love of power and money also continue to drive us too often to favor the few over the interests of the common good. History and personal observations easily reveal that instilling or allowing excessive power and money into the wrong hands will lead to corruption and chaos and nothing good. Such an environment restricts our movement toward a better quality of life which we all seek and prefer to enjoy. Yet, I believe things can change for the better; I have kept the faith – in things hoped for and the evidence of things not yet seen.

Inequities continue to persist in many areas in our country including, in particular: income; housing options; jobs; education; exposure to museums; opportunities to enjoy the arts; health care; and travel. In some states and communities, large segments of the population believe they are discouraged from voting rather than welcomed to exercise democracy in elections. No doubt the common good will be better served when we operate on more of a "level playing field" mentality in each one of these and other areas, where all are treated with common humanitarian approaches and when the old habits of the past have disappeared. Whether consciously or unconsciously, inequities exist in the United States and other countries. Not enough has been done in national, state, and local legislation and practices to take the dramatic steps needed to grow beyond the ills of segregation, racism, and classism of the past. We would all be better served to adjust, prepare, and encourage those of color and the poor to have an equal opportunity to succeed.

There remains much to do to make up for past laws and practices to move us more strongly toward an atmosphere of fully sharing the benefits of freedom and liberty our nation offers to some but not to all.

Among other injustices and unfair practices, the opportunities for jobs continue to favor the majority population over those who have for years faced subjugation and blockage from educational advancement and, thereby, adequate preparation and positioning for equal opportunities for the positions of power and wealth. The advantages of position power place limits on opportunities for some while offering better job options for others. When relatives and friends gain employment in positions of power and authority, they are often motivated to hire or influence the hiring of others of their preference. Poverty is an obvious outcome associated with long struggles to secure adequate employment opportunities with little or no success. Lack of a high-quality education only contributes to the problem by lessening the potential for selection to advanced level employment positions. I still believe things can change for the better; I have kept the faith – in things hoped for and the evidence of things not yet seen.

If, for example, there is a race of two people from one place to another of ten miles in distance, and one person travels in a brand new luxury automobile, and the other travels on a brand new bicycle or is walking the distance, the person traveling in the automobile will win every time. Such is the case of living standards in comparing the "haves" lifestyle with the "have nots" and the highly educated with the highly uneducated. Yet, we compare people of different economic backgrounds and races as though the "playing field" were fair and level. The fact is things are not so fair and level; although, more level than many years ago. It is real that people of all races often see and react to things through a "race based", "colored" or "class based" lens. The glass is too full of same as usual. Let us get a "taller" glass, thereby, improving the outlook for a more positive quality of life for all. Indeed, let us work toward a race and class consciousness to create a wider reach of opportunities for all. We can all benefit from practicing the principles of the Winners Always Practice Program, as summarized in this text, which offers ideas for a common-sense approach to living a more righteous, fair, and balanced lifestyle.

We should all be careful about stereotyping people based upon our perceptions and pre-conceived notions of reality. There are wonderful people who are nice, intelligent, respectful, and caring and live according to a faith-based orientation. I am convinced they are part of the great majority of people. There are also some other people who are not so nice, respectful, and caring, and they do not live in accordance with faith-based principles. Both groups are represented by people of all races. It is not appropriate or even rational to target which group a person better identifies with, based upon his or her race. Think about being alone at night walking toward a group of unfamiliar faces. It should not matter the color of skin whether you feel safe. What about spending time in a public library or a coffee shop with "Wi-Fi" technology capabilities, with plans to study or prepare for a presentation and you hear a noise which distracts you? Those making the noise are hidden from view. Do you assume the color of those making the noise before you see them? Hopefully not. When a crime occurs, are you one of those who is caught making assumptions about the color of the person who committed the crime? Again, hopefully not. Far too often the stereotypical reaction or response is based upon attitudes about race. Even when persons of color demonstrate the highest levels of success and accomplishments, some are prone to think in backwards terms instead of pushing forward in their perceptions and thinking about persons of a different race. Consider, for example, how a superintendent of schools in the Houston, Texas, area lost his job after making ridiculous, negative, and racially charged comments on social media. He wrote "You cannot count on a black quarterback," referring to the Black quarterback of the Houston Texans football team. He later apologized but only after he had been publicly "outed" and criticized about his opinions regarding race and class. This situation happened not in 1864 or in 1918, but in 2018. We still have a long way to go in our thinking about issues of race, and this is but one example. Things can and must change for the better; I have kept the faith – in things hoped for and the evidence of things not yet seen.

The application of justice is affected by race and class, and people are often hypocritical about their own beliefs and actions. A person's color and income status should not be the determining factor on how a situation is addressed, but that is routinely how things are handled. People tend to think about or react to an issue depending upon the advantages or disadvantages to them, personally or professionally. They may take one position one day and a different position when they believe what they prefer may delay or block or influence what they would prefer to happen for their own benefit. The priority is different or changed based upon effect on them or their associates. The concept of double standards goes beyond a term or concept; it is a real issue. Take, for example, situations where a young person of color is charged with a minor law offense and in court faces punishment of a major fine and possible time in jail. When a person not of color is charged with the same minor law offense, the data show that chances of his or her facing the same punishment is doubtful. Note the following findings of inequality in applying justice:

1. Consistent with its previous reports, the Commission found that sentence length continues to be associated with some demographic factors. In particular, after controlling for a wide variety of sentencing variables, the Commission found: Black male offenders continued to receive longer sentences than similarly situated White male offenders...Black men serve sentences that are on the average 19.1 percent longer than those for white men for similar crimes. (King, E. Y. November, 2017. Black men get longer prison sentences than white men for the same crime: Study – Demographic Differences in Sentencing: An Update to the 2012 Booker Report.)

2. African Americans are more likely than white Americans to be arrested: once arrested, they are more likely to be convicted; and once convicted, they are more likely to experience lengthy prison sentences. African American adults are 5.9 times as likely to be incarcerated than whites. (The Sentencing Project report of the U. S. Sentencing Commission submitted to the United Nations Special Rapporteur on Contemporary Forms of Racism, Racial Discrimination, Xenophobia, and Related Intolerance April, 2018)

Too often it is about who you know, income status and race. A leader must learn and practice skills aligned with honor, integrity, truthfulness, fairness and equitable treatment of all and then "Let it go!" Move on to the next issue.

People want to get their way, above all else, in many instances. Where does truth fit into it? Where is the fairness principle in determining how best to proceed on an issue? When does consistency matter, and how does the concept of equity influence things? Are there disparities in how authorities address situations, where the data reflect differences in how people are treated according to their race and income status? Yes. Study after study has revealed inequities and inappropriate actions by authorities in schools and the criminal justice system where the punishments imposed are different, where people of color suffer more serious consequences than other people. In environments where there is a concentration of low income and minority populations, the data show that authorities tend to mete out harsher punishments than what happens in those environments mixed more heavily with people not of color and those of upper income status. Again, this reality is reflective inside and outside school environments, in communities within and across the United States and in other countries.

Profiling occurs within and across all types of neighborhoods, low-income to high. I know this from personal experience, even after achieving education success at the highest level achievable in education -- Doctor of Philosophy -- and professional success as teacher and administrator, including that of serving as superintendent. Two examples follow: (a) I was stopped by a police officer early one evening in the state of Georgia about one mile from my home which was a genuinely nice middle-class neighborhood. The officer asked me for my name and to take my license out of my pocket for him to see. I asked the reason for being pulled over, and his answer was that he was just checking the reason why I was driving in that neighborhood -- racial profiling, for sure; (b) as mentioned in the book previously, I was detained by an officer near a bank in central Texas, not a long distance from the site of my birth family. He demanded that I show my license and explain what I was doing near the bank. I had just used the bank's automated teller machine. I was offended and told him so and contacted the local police department supervisor of the officer and complained. The supervisor explained that he would counsel with the officer about how to better handle such a situation in the future. Good time to "Let it go!" Move on to the next issue.

Consider a report by researchers from The University of Virginia, published in the proceedings of the National Academy of Sciences of The United States of America where they reported that in quizzing White medical students and medical residents, they discovered that as many as half of the study participants held false beliefs, such as African Americans had less sensitive nerve endings than Whites, that African Americans' blood coagulates more quickly, that the skin of African Americans was thicker than that of Whites, and more. The study revealed that Whites were more likely to be prescribed stronger pain medications for similar or equivalent ailments because of the belief that black people have a higher pain tolerance. (PNAS. April 4, 2016. Racial bias in pain assessment and treatment recommendations, and false beliefs about biological differences between Blacks and Whites).

At times we tend to either ignore or misinterpret the effect of certain conditions, such as environmental racism, poverty and lack of education and job opportunities. All these conditions matter and can become "game changers" in the sense of being disabling factors and denial of a sense of hope. Lack of education is a huge and life-long disabling factor and affects every aspect of life for a lifetime. When we educate our citizens, we all benefit. The sense of hope increases beyond measure and moves one to an attitude of hope as well as encouragement of the opportunities for happiness and success. The multiplying effect is tremendous when we successfully educate all our citizens and give everyone a better opportunity to be a productive citizen. Thereby, we enable improvement in the conditions for democracy and higher quality of life. Finally, image matters -- how it looks and how people are made to look or feel makes a difference, including on issues of race. All people matter and deserve to be treated with respect and dignity, and no one deserves to be mistreated or disrespected because of their race, class, or otherwise. We do ourselves a favor in this great nation to see everyone as important and deserving of appreciation for our individual differences, as we are all truly equally unique and valuable human beings. We should celebrate diversity and not resist it.

I am most proud of and thankful for the hard work, sacrifices, and extraordinary patience demonstrated by many of the civil rights leaders of our time. I enjoyed the pleasure of meeting some of these leaders and learned much about thinking strategically, keeping the "end in mind" and not to be distracted by mid-course and early instances of interruptions to the stated mission. I remain committed to following the model set by these leaders in demonstrating humility and showing tendencies of being humble over arrogance. Whether in meetings or in church settings or in one-on-one conversations, the civil rights leaders I had the pleasure of being around while living in Birmingham, Alabama and Metro-Atlanta, Georgia were humble -- would stop and speak with any and all and never showed disrespect or disregard for others. They did not act as though they were superior to or more important than others. Each of them articulated in an eloquent, inspirational manner their ideas denouncing racism and inequality and the effects of both on their victims. They often spoke provocatively of the need to change the conditions that would improve the quality of life for all humanity. While living in the state of Georgia, Carolyn and I attended programs featuring speakers with lively conversations about race, class, and equality, including Minister Louis Farrakhan, considered by many to be polemical in his approach and style of speaking. I was proud of and thankful for the opportunities to participate in programs and knowing the wife of civil rights leader, Dr. Martin Luther King, Jr., Mrs. Coretta Scott King, the King children, and other King family members. Also, I am proud of the opportunities I enjoyed to know and be in meetings with other civil rights leaders, such as Reverend Joseph E. Lowery, Reverend Jesse Jackson, Reverend Al Sharpton, Mr. Shelley Stewart, Reverend Fred Shuttlesworth, Ambassador Andrew Young, Reverend C. T. Vivian, Congressman John Lewis, Reverend Abraham Woods, Jr., Reverend James Orange, Reverend John Porter, local, national and NAACP leaders, Rainbow Coalition representatives, Southern Christian Leadership Conference members, and others.

I found the faith-based community to be one of the most important groups to work with in support of educating our children. Thousands of grade school aged children and their parents attend church, and they communicate routinely with their pastors on important issues, including education. I thoroughly enjoyed the school-church partnerships as education leader, especially attending the advisory committee meetings with the pastors and visiting the churches in the community. I also enjoyed the various ceremonies related to the civil rights movement, such as the Martin Luther King, Jr. Day Holiday Celebrations in Birmingham with a full day of activities. Each year the day started with the annual community breakfast, followed by a parade, starting downtown, and ending with a church rally at one of the popular iconic churches, usually the 16th Street Baptist Church. The community breakfast activities and phenomenal choir included members from different school districts, churches, and other organizations -- Black, White, Latinx, Jewish, and others. The parade included civil rights leaders, high school bands and community members. We sang freedom spiritual/gospel songs such as, Ain't Gonna Let Nobody Turn Me 'Round. LYRICS FOLLOW:

> *Ain't gonna let nobody*
> *Turn me 'round*
> *Turn me 'round*
> *Turn me 'round*
> *Ain't gonna let nobody*
> *Turn me round*
> *I'm gonna keep on walkin'*
> *Keep on talkin'*
> *Marchin' into freedom land.*

The work of these "giants" and others in the areas of civil and human rights has proven that things can and have changed for the better. I observed such work by these civil rights leaders up close and personal in many settings: churches; hotels; auditoriums; community town hall meetings; and school – church partnership meetings. One proud and remarkable example of leadership I observed was through the weekly meetings of the Georgia Coalition for the People's Agenda, the convener of which was the Reverend Dr. Joseph E. Lowery. The meeting always included politicians and representatives from the public who cared to attend and civil rights leaders of Georgia and national prominence. The agenda was basic and targeted issues, such as voting empowerment, education, criminal injustice, and environmental justice. I also appreciated being in meetings and programs led by the Reverend Jesse Jackson, including the opportunity to travel with him in his motorcade from a luncheon in Birmingham to one of the schools where he was to speak. Additionally, I had an extraordinary opportunity to join him in a meeting in New York City at one of the annual Rainbow/ PUSH meetings, sponsored by some of the major companies of our nation. Rainbow/PUSH was formed as a merger of two organizations founded by Reverend Jackson—Operation PUSH and the National Rainbow Coalition, focused on the pursuit of social justice, civil rights, and political activism. Through it all, I have kept the faith – in things hoped for and the evidence of things not yet seen.

Chapter Nine

Winners Always Practice Program

The following presentation is an offering of ideas which may be beneficial for all, from childhood through adulthood, starting with a list of 21 components to consider which, when practiced, will add joy and value to each day: Winners Always Practice Program (WAPP), followed by a list of 9 "plus 1" keys to victory in business and school organizations. The chapter continues with a list of critical issues to address in reform and change for improvement and, finally, a summary of those areas which are critical to focus on to make the greatest difference in governance, leadership and more in school districts.

In an effort to be brief and "to the point" on comments regarding ideas and strategies for improvement through the WAPP, I deliberately limited the explanations to brief comments per category, with full intent to elaborate further in future editions of this and other books. All categories are important, and "connecting the dots" within and across each category makes a tremendous difference.

WINNERS ALWAYS PRACTICE PROGRAM (WAPP): "TEAMWORK MAKES THE DREAM WORK"! THINK "TEAM" AND THINK AND ACT LIKE CHAMPIONS, ALWAYS.

Twenty-one easy-to-address behaviors, practices, qualities and areas of growth and development to win -- in sports and life. By practicing all day everyday each of these categories and components, the chances to win increases in all phases of life, sports, school and for getting along with others within and across race, class and otherwise. Yes, we can all succeed and get along with others, if we wish, by taking time to practice the following well established and accepted behaviors.

Winners Always Practice Program (WAPP) summaries, in common terms and examples of biblical passages for alignment and representation of biblical perspective per component, with all passages from The King James Version Study Bible (KJV). Copyright 1988, 2013, 2017 by Liberty University. The King James Study Bible. Publisher: Thomas Nelson, a registered trademark of HarperCollins Christian Publishing, Inc. General Editor: Edward E. Hindson. Some Bible verses were deliberately applied to more than one WAPP concept for reference and alignment.

- Common sense - Common sense relates to natural tendencies and knowledge based upon routine growth experiences. The information "bank" to "pull from" or benefit from is common to all, and special training and experiences are not required for reference in determining how best to behave. Or, stated in more common terms, act as if you are smart or well trained and dignified, especially, if others are around or may be affected by your behavior. Always avoid behaving "stupidly" when it is just as easy to behave "smartly." Practice!

  ➢ *Alignment with Bible Passages*:
  "Be not deceived: evil communications corrupt good manners." (1 Corinthians 15: 33)

  "But be ye doers of the word, and not hearers only, deceiving your own selves. For if any be a hearer of the word, and not a doer, he is like unto a man beholding his natural face in a glass: For he beholdeth himself, and goeth his way, and straightway forgetteth what manner of man he was. But whoso looketh into the perfect law of liberty, and continueth *therein*, he being not a forgetful hearer, but a doer of the work, this man shall be blessed in his deed." (James 1: 22-25)

"For wisdom *is* better than rubies; and all the things that may be desired are not to be compared to it" (Proverbs 8: 11)

"If thou be wise, thou shalt be wise for thyself: but *if* thou scornest, thou alone shalt bear it." (Proverbs 9: 12)

"Wise *men* lay up knowledge: but the mouth of the foolish *is* near destruction." (Proverbs 10: 14)

"It *is* as sport to a fool to do mischief: but a man of understanding hath wisdom." (Proverbs 10: 23)

"The tongue of the wise useth knowledge aright: but the mouth of fools poureth out foolishness." (Proverbs 15: 2)

"The lips of the wise disperse knowledge: but the heart of the foolish *doeth* not so." (Proverbs 15: 7)

"Folly *is* joy to *him* that *is* destitute of wisdom: but a man of understanding walketh uprightly." (Proverbs 15: 21)

"The heart of the righteous studieth to answer: but the mouth of the wicked poureth out evil things." (Proverbs 15: 28)

Reflection(s): "Let it go!" Let nothing and no one get in the way of your march toward greater success, and always remain goal directed and focused on "winning the game". Make sure all the "dots connect" in a rational manner and avoid blockages of progress by others or yourself. In stressful, tense, and emotional situations, time to practice What to Say, When to Say it, and When to stop talking (WWWST) concepts by using your head, not your mouth until you calm down. Practice: "Let it go!" *These thoughts are used as a foundational statement that appears in each of the principles presented in this chapter.*

It takes only common sense to understand that the best way to enjoy a high-quality life is to focus on what matters most for good health and well-being for self and family. Therefore, the only time left for interacting with other people is for reaching out to help them, not to distract or bother them in an unwelcomed manner. Whether the setting is in a personal circumstance or in public, it is important to learn to walk away when things appear to get heated, conflictual, or uncomfortable. It is so very disappointing to hear of situations connected to behaviors where someone complains of their "space" being violated, or they complain of someone bothering them in some unwelcomed way. Most of the time it pertains to reports of males being accused of some unacceptable behavior at the high school or college/university level. Sometimes groups are involved in or witness the behavior being reported. Of course, these cases involve women aggressors as well. Stop it before it starts! Stop it! Stop it! Use common sense. Enjoy life in a lane of peace and joy for self, family and help others do the same -- mind your own business. Think, plan, act on what is right, comfortable, and joyful every second of each day.

I suggest setting up straight talk sessions which include group vignettes, action plays or theatrical activities to illustrate or mimic to our youth various challenges and how best to handle situations which they may encounter. Dramas and other types of simulations can be used to address sensitive issues, such as the following: illicit drugs or alcohol possession or use; weapons showing up unexpectantly; private matters that may involve intimacy; fighting or other impending altercations and conflicts; lack of school success; depression; problems with peers; and other social-emotional issues of today's youth.

It is also simply application of common sense to understand that what we think and believe and the actions we take will lead toward or away from the results we expect. For example, if we want to become a high school or college/university graduate, we must enroll in and attend school and complete coursework successfully. If one wants to avoid jail time, follow the law, and do the right things. If a person wishes to become an electrician, complete the requisite training, and so on. It's all about common sense and focusing on doing things at the right time and in the right way. Always remember to compare the risks with the anticipated rewards.

Those who are most successful plan and work hard for the desired outcomes. If you wish to be promoted in your organization, it is commonly understood that the way to best position yourself is to work hard, demonstrate leadership by example, focus on and be successful at your work assignment, get along with other employees, show up on time, show willingness to go beyond what is required, show you are dependable, show that the company management can consistently count on you. Always have an "own the store" mentality and apply your common sense to every action you take at home or work.

Everybody wants to win, period! The concept of winning applies in multiple angles: sports, work, contracts and more. In life it is more likely than not that one cannot and will not win first place every time desired, no matter how much preparation or degree of intensity in the efforts. There is, however, a difference in not winning first place and defeat. The positive way to look at not winning first place is to analyze what went correctly and what could have gone better and to learn and grow from it and go out and try again. Another way to view not winning is to complain, pout, whine, blame everyone and everything other than those things over which you had control and then quit. In that case you are showing signs of being defeated. I enjoyed the days of my competing as an athlete, including my participation in middle school in football, basketball and track and high school in track and football for only one year and basketball for four years. I served as the high school captain of the team as a senior and played basketball in college. I remain clear that the right attitude to display when you win first place is to show appreciation and that you are humble and grateful for such an honor.

Winning requires understanding what it is you are competing for as well as degrees of the win. Winning goes beyond winning first place. For example, a track runner in the 100 meter dash who runs a race and comes in last out of eight runners in one race and follows in the next race against the same group and comes in fifth place can rightfully declare himself or herself as winning through making excellent progress. I recall meeting three high school track runners and their parents at a local university on the running track who were training for the state high school track meet in Texas which was two weeks away. I met one athlete Friday evening and the other two Saturday morning. Each had won first place or second place in the local district and regional track meets in Southeast Texas. They were working hard to be prepared for the state meet and being mentored primarily by their fathers -- thank God for fathers and mothers who will spend their time in this manner. I asked each athlete whether other runners on their school teams had qualified for the state track meet, and the athletes and fathers answered, "Yes". One indicated that she had practiced earlier at the high school the same day. However, after she completed the regularly scheduled practice at the high school, she thought it important to dedicate additional time to practice on her own. She was, therefore, going beyond the regular practice program to prepare for the upcoming state track meet. The other two student athletes also spent time working hard to prepare, beyond the regular high school required practice schedule. In my view, these athletes were already winners, several days prior to the actual state track meet for the state of Texas, sponsored by the University Interscholastic League Organization.

Interestingly, but not surprisingly, the star athletes competing at the high school, college, and professional levels are well acquainted and know the accomplishments of their competitors within the state and on a national basis, ladies, and men. In the eyes of these high school athletes and of their fathers, they were not satisfied with just being invited to participate. They were winners who reflected the importance of "always practicing"—fine models of the Winners Always Practice Program. They were also demonstrating common sense; that is, if you want to win, you must practice and not just show up and expect success.

The concept works in adulthood as well. If you want the job or the contract, you must prepare and often outperform others. Therefore, common sense tells you that you may have to devote more time and attention than others or go to school longer in preparation to gain the victory.

There is one additional point to convey regarding the sport of track, and I believe it takes only common sense to address the concern. That is, competitors who compete in running events are not allowed, even, one false start in avoiding disqualification. This rule is preposterous and

114

unreasonable, and it is the only team sport where individuals and entire relay teams are disqualified for such a mistake -- of starting the race too fast. Yet, if you fail to start fast you have much less chance to win the race. In basketball, for example, you can overcome a mistake from start until the final seconds of the contest. It is the same in football, soccer, baseball, softball, and all other team sports. In the past the rule allowed up to two false starts, resulting in some races taking much longer in time to complete the race. Obviously, the faster you get started affects your ability to finish the race faster than the other runners, especially in the speed races. It is most perplexing that this "no false start" rule is applied even at the level of championship track meets, that is, district, regional, state, and national track meets. The rule is more of a convenience for adults who attend and work at the track meets. It is not enforced in consideration of the student athletes and should be modified to at least allow one false start per racing event prior to disqualification.

The student athlete practices for the entire season and longer for those who practice in advance of the season. The persons charged with management of the start of the races are different in each track meet, thereby, different mannerisms, speed and cadence in giving the start of the race commands, making it difficult to anticipate how swiftly to get started in the race. If you wait too long to start, you have little to no chance to win, and if you start too fast in anticipating when the race will start -- even one time -- you are disqualified. I can recall in the case of the Texas regional track meets I attended for several years in the Metro-Houston area, the person managing the start of the races was a person who had apparently earned what appeared to be the right for a lifetime commitment to serve as the starter. He was especially slow in his commands and in using the starter pistol for the start of races. Unfortunately, it has been routine for individual runners and relay teams to be disqualified for starting their races too fast or making any movements prior to the starting "pistol" being heard. Many, many complained to no avail, and year after year the same shameful and regrettable impact on the youth has been experienced. So, who are the advocates for track competitors for changes in this rule? Hopefully, the parents and those track coaches who are serious about coaching in the sport are prime to show such advocacy.

Many high school track coaches consider the coaching assignment to be a secondary assignment, with the primary assignment being that of coaching football or possibly basketball. But even those who may look upon track as a secondary sport, it becomes a priority when faced with the reality of losing the chance to compete in a race due to the runner or relay team facing disqualification because of one false start where the starter is not effective.

Getting back to common sense, it is common sense to know that everyone deserves and expects to be treated with dignity and respect. Yet, it is far too routine to find conflict around issues of one's race, level of income or class in human interactions. It is common sense and fact that when a child is born, intellect is not determined based upon race or environment. Things happen from the first day of birth through an accumulation of events, level of care and attention and environment which contribute in molding intellectual growth and development. Therefore, the so-called gaps in achievement as manifested in test scores among races and other child groupings occur following birth, based upon several factors, such as a child's circumstances--environmental conditions and access to proper health care, whether plentiful reading materials are available with consistent opportunities to read and having someone read to them, exposure to the arts, sophistication and routine use of appropriate grammar and high level verbal and visual cues and language in communication among adults and older children, local and not so local travel experiences, proper nutrition, models on the importance of academic and social advancement, and more.

In growing up while living on Emerson Street the other neighborhood children and I walked to visit nearby neighborhoods and children of our same age group. The differences were stark in comparisons of wealth and access to opportunities between our immediate neighborhood group and the White children from the more affluent areas of the community. We got along well, and communication was friendly. The visits, however, stopped at the doorsteps of our homes, seldom including an invitation or interest in going inside. Yet, we all sought the same things in terms of joy and quality of life; there were more similarities than differences in our character and interests in happiness and being successful in school and other areas of life. We did well to navigate our paths to enjoy the similarities and did not allow differences in race and class or income levels to dictate our ability to get along. Practice!

Reader - Think; Share; Reflect:_____

_____

- Continuous improvement - No one is perfect, and everyone can and should strive to improve. Part of the human growth and development experience is that natural changes occur over which we have no control. Regarding those things over which we do have control, it is imperative to plan for and take advantage of opportunities to improve, within and across all forms of knowledge and conduct. It is safe to say that a person is on the incline in growth and development or in decline, as nothing in the human existence remains the same, over time. Never, ever give up or quit. Practice!

  ➢ *Alignment with Bible Passages*:

    "But let every man prove his own work, and then shall he have rejoicing in himself alone, and not in another. For every man shall bear his own burden." (Galatians 6: 4-5)

    "Give *instruction* to a wise *man*, and he will be yet wiser: teach a just *man*, and he will increase in learning." (Proverbs: 9: 9)

    "Whoso loveth instruction loveth knowledge: but he that hateth reproof *is* brutish." (Proverbs 12: 1)

    "Train up a child in the way he should go: and when he is old, he will not depart from it." Proverbs 22: 6)

    "I can do all things through Christ which strengtheneth me." (Phillipians 4: 13)

"But they that wait upon the LORD shall renew *their* strength; they shall mount up with wings as eagles; they shall run, and not be weary; *and* they shall walk, and not faint." (Isaiah 40: 31)

"For that which I do I allow not: for what I would, that do I not; but what I hate, that do I. If then I do that which I would not, I consent unto the law that *it is* good. Now then it is no more I that do it, but sin that dwelleth in me." (Romans 7:15-17)

"I will instruct thee and teach thee in the way which thou shalt go: I will guide thee with mine eye." (Psalm 32: 8)

"When I was a child, I spake as a child, I understood as a child, I thought as a child: but when I became a man, I put away childish things." (1 Corinthians 13: 11)

"But let patience have *her* perfect work, that ye may be perfect and entire, wanting nothing. If any of you lack wisdom, let him ask of God, that giveth to all *men* literally, and upbraideth not; and it shall be given him." (James 1: 4-5)

Reflection(s): "Let it go!" Let nothing and no one get in the way of your march toward greater success, and always remain goal directed and focused on "winning the game". Make sure all the "dots connect" in a rational manner and avoid blockages of progress by others or yourself. In stressful, tense, and emotional situations, time to practice WWWST concepts by using your head, not your mouth until you calm down. Practice: "Let it go!"

There is no easy ride toward victory; you must work for it. Whether the activity is reading, delivering speeches or presentations, working on the job, riding a bicycle or other physical activities, the more you practice, the opportunity for improvement increases. Stop practicing and you decline in skills and reduce, if not eliminate, the potential for improvement. "Use it or lose it."

I can recall numerous stories of the "march toward excellence", going back to childhood, on how individuals, in general, and athletic teams moved from the performance level of mediocre or average to the "top of the class" in their sport. Examples follow:

- High school and college classmates who devoted time after school, weekends and summers practicing their sport, reading, and studying, moving on to win scholarships for college and contracts in professional sports and toward successful careers, spanning all forms of disciplines.

- Perennial athletics and professional championship teams who win and compete successfully year in and out at the high school, college, and professional levels in all sports. How does this happen? They work hard at continuous improvement, and they focus on teamwork and achieving their mission -- not some of the time, but all the time.

- Artists such as Itzhak Perlman, a famous and phenomenally successful violinist and conductor, I had the pleasure to meet and enjoy one of his performances at Lamar University. He was most humble throughout the performance and in conversation about his remarkable success and how practicing made the greatest difference in his rise to the "top" as a violinist. Perlman, who was born in Tel Aviv, contracted polio at a young age but did not let that stop him in his march toward success. When I met him, he used a scooter and crutches to aide in his mobility but made no excuses and did not complain about the relevant challenges in movement. When asked about what had made the greatest difference in his success, beyond the encouragement from his parents, he pointed to how much he practiced, practiced, practiced to continuously improve in his skills.

- I recall playing a racquetball game at The University of Texas at Austin against a lady who was much younger than I and shorter. She won each game by large margins, and it was an embarrassing experience. In leaving the gym she reminded me to think of the "glass as half full" and not "half empty" and that practicing will make the difference in improving my skills in the sport. She was right and in time upon a lot more practice,

I improved my skills in every aspect of the game, including thinking strategically about where to hit the ball and how to keep the ball low in hitting it off the wall, making it harder for the opponent to respond.

- I was honored and pleased to attend a ballet performance of "super" ballerina, Misty Copeland, in Costa Mesa, California in 2015: The Nutcracker. Ms. Copeland was the first African American dancer named as a principal dancer with the American Ballet Theatre. Carolyn and I enjoyed the pleasure of meeting and speaking briefly with her backstage following the program. All performers did an excellent job, and Ms. Copeland was outstanding in performing her role in the production. Coincidentally, we had enjoyed lunch at a restaurant near the theatre -- Segerstrom Center for The Arts--and met some of the youth who also were part of the program. They explained that they were part of the team traveling and performing as part of the American Ballet Theatre program and were excited to perform with Misty. The youth and Misty Copeland spoke of and demonstrated in their performance the importance of practicing to perfect the skills required to perform successfully.

Think of the best performers for any activity or job and ask the question of how they attained the skills for achieving at that level. No doubt, they practiced, practiced, practiced, and exhibited extraordinary passion for achievement. This point holds true in sports and every other activity. The lazy and those who refuse to put in the time and demonstrate the commitment and passion for continuous improvement cannot achieve at the best of anything. This point is transferable regardless of the activity. In one real-life, important example that affects the growth and development of children and quality of life, reading, reading, reading consistently several hours per day results in improved reading skills, including comprehension, recognizing, and understanding words and increasing knowledge.

Never give up. So often the victory is just beyond the temptation to quit. In fact, one of the enemies of victory is not to try at all. It has been said that you cannot get to second base in baseball if you keep your feet on first base. Likewise, if you want to know what is in the book, you must first open it, and so on. This logic works in all fields or endeavors. For example, as education leader and civil rights advocate, I have worked hard to ensure that children enjoy learning in facilities which are appropriate and comparable to those considered to be among the finest. Our children deserve the nicest environments to learn in regardless of which neighborhood they live in and their zip code. I have made deliberate attempts to go beyond the words in my commitment on facilities.

The challenges may be great for achieving something extraordinary, but that is no excuse not to try to succeed. Examples follow:

- Austin, Texas - The University of Texas at Austin -- The completion of the doctorate was an amazing opportunity, including the networking among the school cohort group of students who had come from varied, diverse backgrounds and experiences. It took several tries before I was accepted into the program. But I did not allow the challenges for getting into the school affect the outcome of my getting out and earning the Doctor of Philosophy degree. I was proud to graduate with straight "A" s in my coursework, including a perfect score in the two-day writing examination finals before graduation. Such success was only possible because I had worked hard and practiced each day on continuous improvement. Practice!

- Birmingham, Alabama -- The school district had not built a new high school in more than 30 years upon my selection as superintendent. Working with the City of Birmingham and State of Alabama officials, the School Board and I set about replacing the original Carver High School with the George Washington Carver High School for Health Professions, Engineering and Technology. We started with the vision for building this new school and several others, while renovating campuses where renovation was sufficient. Upgrading technology in all schools was also a major part of the plan. We were successful in getting it all done! We kept the faith and did not give up.

- Port Arthur, Texas – The community passed a bond issue which included providing funds for building a new high school prior to my tenure as superintendent. Several years later, no movement was made for achieving the vision because of confusion and disagreements about the intended site of the new building. After years of delay, the impact of inflation blocked the opportunity to proceed, as the architectural drawings were already completed, but the funds available were insufficient for completing the project. I was fortunate upon my selection as superintendent to provide administrative leadership in coordination with the school board to determine the appropriate school site and for raising the additional bond funds through approval of the community to get the job done. We were successful in building the beautiful Memorial High School. We did not give up, and by working together, we were able to improve the educational environment for the children for this school and all others in the school district.

Reader - Think; Share; Reflect: _____

_____

- Discipline - Self-discipline is about making choices that are controlled by only one person, that is you! It is one of the most important decisions and, yet, too often one of the most challenging to manage. When managed effectively you stay out of trouble and avoid being confronted with problems and circumstances which can easily become a distraction and block progress toward happiness and well-being. Practice!

➢ *Alignment with Bible Passages:*

"Now no chastening for the present seemeth to be joyous, but grievous: nevertheless afterward it yieldeth the peaceable fruit of righteousness unto them which are exercised thereby." (Hebrews 12: 11)

"Obey them that have the rule over you, and submit yourselves: for they watch for your souls, as they that must give account, that they may do it with joy, and not with grief: for that *is* unprofitable for you." (Hebrews 13: 17)

"He shall die without instruction; and in the greatness of his folly he shall go astray." (Proverbs 5: 23)

"WHOSO loveth instruction loveth knowledge: but he that hateth reproof *is* brutish. A good *man* obtaineth favour of the LORD: but a man of wicked devices will he condemn. A man shall not be established by wickedness: but the root of the righteous shall not be moved. A virtuous woman *is* a crown to her husband: but she that maketh ashamed *is* as rottenness in his bones. The thoughts of the righteous *are* right: *but* the counsels of the wicked *are* deceit." (Proverbs 12: 1-5)

"He that refuseth instruction despiseth his own soul: but he that heareth reproof getteth understanding." (Proverbs 15: 32)

"Love not sleep, lest thou come to poverty; open thine eyes, *and* thou shalt be satisfied with bread." (Proverbs 20: 13)

"Correct thy son, and he shall give thee rest; yea, he shall give delight unto thy soul. Where *there is* no vision, the people perish: but he that keepeth the law, happy *is* he." (Proverbs 29: 17-18)

"Children, obey your parents in the LORD: for this is right. Honour Thy Father And Mother; which is the first commandment with promise. That it may be well with thee, and thou mayest live long on the earth. And, ye fathers, provoke not your children to wrath: but bring them up in the nurture and admonition of the LORD." (Ephesians 6: 1-4)

"But they that wait upon the LORD shall renew *their* strength; they shall mount up with wings as eagles; they shall run, and not be weary; *and* they shall walk and not faint." (Isaiah 40: 31)

"Know ye not that they which run in a race run all, but one receiveth the prize? So run, that ye may obtain. And every man that striveth for the mastery is temperate in all things. Now they *do it* to obtain a corruptible crown; but we an incorruptible. I therefore so run, not as uncertainly; so fight I, not as one that beateth the air; But I keep under my body, and bring *it* into subjection: lest that by any means, when I have preached to others, I myself should be a castaway." (1 Corinthians 9: 24-27)

Reflection(s): "Let it go!" Let nothing and no one get in the way of your march toward greater success, and always remain goal directed and focused on "winning the game". Make sure all the "dots connect" in a rational manner and avoid blockages of progress by others or yourself. In stressful, tense, and emotional situations, time to practice WWWST concepts by using your head, not your mouth until you calm down. Practice: "Let it go!"

Self-discipline is much easier to think and talk about than to demonstrate. It is so much easier because making the right choice may mean balancing or rejecting the decision on what we may want with the decision on what may be better for us or what we may need. It is always about making choices -- good ones or poor ones that propel our paths toward victory, winning or losing. Discipline spans across and within the other components of the WAPP and can make all the difference in the world in a positive way when the right decision is made. When the wrong or questionable decision is made, it can result in something negative. Making a choice can be so much easier than we sometimes make it. Think about it. For example, in deciding on healthy food choices, you can eat a carrot rather than a potato chip if you feel the urge to eat something with a crunchy sound. On another healthy lifestyle choice, most of us can walk a mile for a portion of the day just as easily as deciding to sit on the couch all day and get little to no exercise that day. You can choose to drink a bottle of water just as easily as deciding to drink a can of soda or alcohol. And it is reasonable to believe that many of those things that otherwise may be important to avoid in large amounts may be useful in moderation. Is it not just as easy to smile as it is to frown during a conversation? What about an advent attitude for giving over pushing to take for oneself or to selfishly focus on self over giving or helping others? Is it not just as easy to be nice as it is to be not so nice or to be mean? If the idea is to win the game or win the contract, it makes more sense to practice with the team and to develop and follow the game plan than to miss practice or not to plan or practice at all. Think of the responsibility to go to a meeting on a workday or go to school during a school day, it makes more sense to go than to look for excuses not to go. Winners not only go where they are expected and required or when the team is counting on them, they act beyond ordinary and excel to achieve at the highest levels. Winners think and act like champions, all the time, which means they also demonstrate a sense of pride and dignity and self-discipline.

During any day, a person routinely is faced with making numerous decisions about what to do. Some choices are easier to deal with than others. In some situations, the decisions hold life or death consequences in the balance. One easy decision for all is never to drink and drive and never to allow a friend to drink and drive. Of course, as importantly never use illegal drugs or allow a friend to use illegal drugs and drive an automobile. In self-discipline it is not only an acceptable practice, it is highly appropriate to think about each decision, whether the decision comports with your intended, well thought out strategy or plan for self-discipline. If you have no plan or strategy in place, today is a good day to start in designing one. Practice!

Reader - Think; Share; Reflect: _____

_____

- Focus - It is so easy to set goals and, yet, much more difficult to focus and set plans for and take the actions that are necessary to achieve them. Focusing entails controlling thoughts and actions to address with laser like attention on what matters the most. To focus is also not allowing distractions that may delay or prevent the outcomes desired. You can always find some reason not to focus and many better reasons to focus and maintain it, regardless of the temptations to do otherwise. Practice!

➢ *Alignment with Bible Passages*:

"Let thine eyes look right on, and let thine eyelids look straight before thee." (Proverbs 4: 25)

"Finally, brethren, whatsoever things are true, whatsoever things *are* honest, whatsoever things *are* just, whatsoever things *are* pure, whatsoever things *are* lovely, whatsoever things *are* of good report; if *there* be any virtue, and if *there* be any praise, think on these things." (Philippians 4: 8)

"When I was a child, I spake like a child, I understood as a child, I thought as a child: but when I became a man, I put away childish things." (1 Corinthians 13: 11)

"For the *kingdom of heaven is* as a man traveling into a far country, *who* called his own servants, and delivered unto them his goods. And unto one he gave five talents, to another two, and to another one, to every man according to his several ability; and straightway took his journey. Then he that had received the five talents went and traded with the same, and made *them* other five talents. And likewise he that *had received* two, he also gained other two. But he that had received one went and digged in the earth, and hid his lord's money." (Matthew 25: 14-18)

"And the LORD answered me, and said, Write the vision, and make *it* plain upon tables, that he may run that readeth it. For the vision *is* yet for an appointed time, but at the end it shall speak, and not lie: though it tarry, wait for it; because it will surely come, it will not tarry." (Habakkuk 2: 2-3)

"Brethen, I count not myself to have apprehended: but *this* one thing I *do*, forgetting those things which are behind, and reaching forth unto those things which are before." (Philippians 3: 13)

"Now faith is the substance of things hoped for, the evidence of things not seen." (Hebrews 11: 1)

"And I sent messengers unto them, saying, I *am* doing great work, so that I cannot come down: why should the work cease, whilst I leave it, and come down to you?" (Nehemiah 6: 3)

"Set your affection on things above, not on things on the earth." (Colossians 3: 2)

"Whatsoever thy hand findeth to do, do *it* with thy might; for *there is* no work, nor device, nor knowledge, nor wisdom, in the grave, whither thou goest." (Ecclesiastes 9: 10)

Reflection(s): "Let it go!" Let nothing and no one get in the way of your march toward greater success, and always remain goal directed and focused on "winning the game". Make sure all the "dots connect" in a rational manner and avoid blockages of progress by others or yourself. In stressful, tense, and emotional situations, time to practice WWWST concepts by using your head, not your mouth until you calm down. Practice: "Let it go!"

It is especially important to focus, and it is your decision whether to maintain a positive attitude, especially in stressful situations. The only difference is your attitude which you alone can manage and control. In fact, it is a waste of time focusing on those things over which you have little to no control, and it is essential to recognize that your attitude is one of those things you do control, 100% of the time. It is far better to maintain a positive attitude and treat others with a sense of hospitality and not ever allow yourself to drift into a lane of any appearance of being mean or "messing with people". Always remain focused on achieving the victory you set out to achieve and avoid distractions which may impede your progress. Look at champions of any sport or any avenue of life and what you will find are those individuals who have set goals. They also demonstrate the ability to avoid those things that are not important. They set their minds on what matters and zoom in with laser like focus. Winners know that the path to victory is often not an easy one. Note, it is not coincidental that those who win consistently are repeaters in winning, such as the New England Patriots in professional football or Alabama and Clemson Universities in college football. Other notable examples include Simone Biles in gymnastics, Michael Jordan, Kareem Abdul Jabbar and Kobe Bryant in professional basketball. Whether the game or sport or avenue of life is about victory by an individual or team or company, the same people often repeat as winners. First, they believe in themselves and their plan of operations. They set goals and objectives and keep those in mind. The indicators of success and winning strategies are posted and adhered to. They work hard for the victory, and they focus on doing the little things and big things to "play to win". You cannot be almost focused and win. Close is just not good enough.

Think of the many scenarios where focusing matters, whether in sports or work or regular flow of life. It is extremely easy to become distracted or lazy and mindless for the moment. Yet, think about it; it may take only a moment of losing focus that can result in a life-threatening circumstance: while driving; cooking; delivering an important speech; taking a paper-pencil test; completing a work assignment; in a game, such as basketball, football or soccer, and the ball is tossed or kicked in your direction -- lose focus and you, literally, can lose the game or, even, a life. True, it does take effort to focus, but it is necessary for success. I can recall, for example, in numerous television and radio shows where I participated in conversations with the host and others, in some cases where there were thousands in the listening and viewing audience. I took extraordinary care to listen and make comments that were appropriate to the situation -- excuses and mistakes not acceptable. In a couple of memorable instances, I was a participant in national broadcasts, one of which was a CNN television program regarding the Dekalb County Schools' student school dress code; another, as noted earlier on the importance of reading, along with the United States Department of Education Secretary of Education, Richard Riley. In another example, I was invited to meet with the President of the United States, George W.

Bush in the White House regarding the pending legislation for the "No Child Left Behind" national schools accountability program. There were only 20 or so of us present, including State Department of Education Commissioners and Secretaries for various states and a couple of local school superintendents, including myself, a few governors, the United States Secretary of Homeland Security, and many media representatives at the news conference. No time to be distracted or having a wandering mindset -- had to focus to be relevant in the conversation and to best serve the children I was there to represent. I also recall the many presentations I delivered for hundreds of people, and even when the audience was small, I was clear that it is important to focus, listen and respond with purpose.

Even when playing in a game like football or basketball, track, tennis, golf, swimming, hockey, soccer and other sports, it is important to think "team" over "self" and to focus during every play: shooting a free throw, or catching a forward pass, or hitting the golf ball, or accepting a pass in soccer, and more. The same holds true for settings such as business and church meetings. Focus! Play to win the game and to succeed. Practice!

Reader - Think; Share; Reflect: _____

_____

- Follow Law - Laws exist for a reason: to protect all from harm, promote democracy and support us all as we seek to enjoy the "common good" and better quality of life. Do what you are supposed to do and not what you are not to do. Always keep the brain "open", and keep the thoughts and actions directed toward advantages for and reasons to follow all laws whether local, state or nationally generated. There is always a possibility of being caught, thereby, bringing negative attention toward you along with penalties which can derail or ruin the "road" to winning on and off the playing field or court. Remember, in the "world" of current technology, officials can find out all kinds of information through review of records from cameras, cell phones, credit cards and banking records. Sooner or later when you fail to follow the law, you will be caught and will face the consequences of your actions. Practice!

> *Alignment with Bible Passages:*

"For not the hearers of the law *are* just before God, but the doers of the law shall be justified." (Romans 2: 13)

"Let every soul be subject unto the higher powers. For there is no power but of God: the powers that be are ordained of God . . . Render therefore to all their dues: tribute to whom tribute *is due*; custom to whom custom; fear to whom fear; honour to whom honour." (Romans 13: 1; 7)

"Put them in mind to be subject to principalities and powers, to obey magistrates, to be ready to every good work." (Titus 3: 1)

"*Is* the law then against the promises of God? God forbid: for if there had been a law given which could have given life, verily righteousness should have been by the law. But the scripture hath concluded all under sin, that the promise by faith of Jesus Christ might be given to them that believe. But before faith came, we were kept under the law, shut up unto the faith which should afterwards be revealed. Wherefore the law was our schoolmaster to *bring us* unto Christ, that we might be justified by faith" (Galatians 3: 21-24)

"But the fruit of the Spirit is love, joy, peace, long-suffering, gentleness, goodness, faith, Meekness, temperance: against such there is no law." (Galatians 5: 22-23)

"They that forsake the law praise the wicked: but such as keep the law contend with them. Evil men understand not judgment: but they that seek the LORD understand all *things*. Better *is* the poor that walketh in his uprightness, than *he that is* perverse *in his* ways, though he *be* rich. Whoso

130

keepeth the law *is* a wise son: but he that is a companion of riotous *men* shameth his father." (Proverbs 28: 4 - 7)

"But the fearful, and unbelieving, and the abominable, and murderers, and whoremongers, and sorcerers and idolators, and all liars, shall have their part in the lake which burneth with fire and brimstone: which *is* the second death." (Revelation 21: 8)

"Blessed *is* the man that walketh not in the counsel of the ungodly, nor standeth in the way of sinners, nor sitteth in the seat of the scornful. But his delight *is* in the law of the LORD; and in his law doth he meditate day and night. And he shall be like a tree planted by the rivers of water, that bringeth forth his fruit in his season; his leaf also shall not wither; and whatsoever he doeth shall prosper. The ungodly *are* not so; but *are* like the chaff which the wind driveth away. Therefore, the ungodly shall not stand in the judgment, nor sinners in the congregation of the righteous. For the LORD knoweth the way of the righteous: but the way of the ungodly shall perish." (Psalm 1: 1 – 6)

"Whosoever committeth sin transgresseth also the law: for sin is the transgression of the law." (1 John 3: 4)

"But whoso looketh into the perfect law of liberty, and continueth *therein*, he being not a forgetful hearer, but a doer of the work, this man shall be blessed in his deed." (James 1: 25)

Reflection(s): "Let it go!" Let nothing and no one get in the way of your march toward greater success, and always remain goal directed and focused on "winning the game". Make sure all the "dots connect" in a rational manner and avoid blockages of progress by others or yourself. In stressful, tense, and emotional situations, time to practice WWWST concepts by using your head, not your mouth until you calm down. Practice: "Let it go!"

No excuses acceptable; follow the law, period! Of course, there may be instances which arise where disputes or lack of understandings lead to legal disputes. And everyone is prone to make mistakes. Yet, where possible, better to keep it simple and do what is easily the right thing to do. When you know the law or question whether something is or is not lawful, err each time on the side of caution and avoidance, so as not to take the chance of your actions being out of line with the law. Do only those things which you know and believe are the right things to do. Look out for your neighbor in helping somebody over doing that which may be harmful to self or others.

Happiness and joy are generally not achievable when contemplating or taking actions which may result in pain and suffering for yourself or others. After all the primary reason that we have laws in place is to serve justice in favor of the common good -- that includes you and all others. The consequences for doing the wrong thing in breaking the law are bothersome for the companies or victims affected by the crime and, ultimately, for the perpetrator when apprehended. It is not worth it even to think crime let alone commit the crime. It is easy to rationalize in your thinking the possible benefits if not caught with the consequences one faces if apprehended. The chances are greater that you will be caught -- then, again, everyone affected is harmed, including you and your family and the persons targeted by your illegal actions. It is just not worth it. Follow the law every day of life. Also, always remember this simple rule: "Don't mess with other people, their property or their money", and life is, therefore, better for you and all others around you. True winners make wise choices and among the wisest of choices one can make is to follow the law -- do what you are supposed to do and not what you are not.

And, always keep in mind the thought: "Leave other people alone!" Practice!

Reader - Think; Share; Reflect: _____

_____

- Healthy lifestyle (no alcohol, drugs, eat right & exercise) - Being healthy is directly affected and driven by lifestyle and choices about eating, drinking, exercising, resting, and intake of substances. Attitude makes a difference realizing, for example, that expending the energy for a smile is far less difficult to develop than to develop a frown, and the impact is more healthful. To smile and seek happiness and acting out such an emotion is a good idea. Remember, how you live your life is your decision and none is more important than to choose to live a healthy lifestyle. Practice!

➤ *Alignment with Bible Passages*:

"Be not wise in thine own eyes: fear the LORD, and depart from evil. It shall be health to thy navel, and marrow to thy bones. Honour the LORD with thy substance, and with the first fruits of all thine increase." *(*Proverbs 3: 7-9)

"A sound heart *is* the life of the flesh: but envy the rottenness of the bones." (Proverbs 14: 30)

"A merry heart doeth good *like* a medicine: but a broken spirit drieth the bones." (Proverbs 17: 22)

"Be not among winebibbers; among riotous eaters of flesh: For the drunkard and the glutton shall come to poverty: and drowsiness shall clothe *a man* with rags." (Proverbs 23: 20-21)

"He giveth power to the faint; and to *them that have* no might he increaseth strength. Even the youths shall faint and be weary, and the young men shall utterly fall: But they that wait upon the LORD shall renew *their* strength; they shall mount up with wings as eagles; they shall run, and not be weary; *and* they shall walk, and not faint." (Isaiah 40: 29-31)

"Beloved, I wish above all things that thou mayest prosper and be in health, even as thy soul prospereth." (3 John 1: 2)

"And God said, Behold, I have given you every herb bearing seed, which *is* upon the face of all the earth, and every tree, in the which *is* the fruit of a tree yielding seed; to you it shall be for meat. And to every beast of the earth, and to every fowl of the air, and to every thing that creepeth upon the earth, wherein *there is* life, I *have given* every green herb for meat: and it was so." (Genesis 1: 29-30)

"Him that *is* weak in the faith receive ye, *but* not to doubtful disputations. For one believeth that he may eat all things: another, who is weak, eateth herbs. Let not him that eateth despise him that eateth not; and let not him which eateth not judge him that eateth: for God hath received him." (Romans 14: 1-3)

"Therefore I say unto you, Take no thought for your life, what ye shall eat, or what ye shall drink; nor yet for your body, what ye shall put on. Is not the life more than meat, and the body than raiment? Behold the fowls of the air: for they sow not, neither do they reap, nor gather into barns; yet your heavenly Father feedeth them. Are ye not much better than they." (Matthew 6: 25-26)

"For bodily exercise profiteth little: but godliness is profitable unto all things, having promise of the life that now is, and of that which is to come." (1 Timothy 4: 8)

Reflection(s): "Let it go!" Let nothing and no one get in the way of your march toward greater success, and always remain goal directed and focused on "winning the game". Make sure all the "dots connect" in a rational manner and avoid blockages of progress by others or yourself. In stressful, tense, and emotional situations, time to practice WWWST concepts by using your head, not your mouth until you calm down. Practice: "Let it go!"

Start today if you have not already figured this out, eat healthy foods, including fruits and vegetables, and eat other foods in moderation and exercise daily. Complicated concept, no -- not at all. Yet, it is apparent from the data and observations all around us that far too many of us do not follow this simple rule. I recall a conversation with an employee at an airport luggage check-in area where the gentleman said that he had waited until he was 60 years old to decide to start eating fruits and vegetables. Too late? No not at all; better late than never, but much better had he and all of us been mindful to start at infancy and maintained the standard through childhood and young adulthood and beyond. It can be done and is necessary for the best possible quality of life and well-being. This is another area where making good choices makes a major difference in whether a person wins for high quality of life or positions oneself for a lifestyle that ensures a path toward problems that are avoidable.

Consider the training regimen and eating and exercise routines of the best athletes during the time of their participation in action sports. The most successful of them eat healthy foods with set schedules and routines, and they exercise, often pushing themselves beyond ordinary for the best results. Some even go so far as hiring nutritionists and trainers for organizing menus and practice schedules. The term "discipline" comes to mind here. Why? Because part of any plan for success requires discipline and psychological edge. If it were easy and anyone could do it, there would be more limited separation between those who succeed and those who do not. Yet, it is possible for each person to enjoy victory in lifestyle and better health by simply making the right decisions and maintaining the discipline as needed to eat properly. That means regular helpings of fruits and vegetables and not going heavy on meats and fried foods and by implementing a schedule of vigorous exercise. Of course, all should get an adequate amount of rest each day and avoid the use of smoking and other drugs and alcohol. Among numerous other important factors for winning in life and enjoying a high quality of life, excellent health practices translate strongly as an especially important factor. Practice!

Reader - Think; Share; Reflect: _____

_____

- Honor (think and act your best with integrity and character) –
  Everyone has a name. That "good" name represents your family,
  self, and history -- past and future. The best way to protect
  that "good" name is to think and act with integrity and strong
  character. Such behavior is expected and preferred in all circles
  of life across the world, characterized by carrying oneself and
  treating others with respect and dignity and in accordance with
  the law and "high" moral character. Practice!

  ➤ *Alignment with Bible Passages*:

  "He that walketh uprightly walketh surely: but he that
  perverteth his ways shall be known." (Proverbs 10: 9)

  "The integrity of the upright shall guide them: but the
  perverseness of transgressors shall destroy them." (Proverbs
  11: 3)

  "The righteousness of the perfect shall direct his way: but the
  wicked shall fall by his own wickedness. The righteousness
  of the upright shall deliver them: but transgressors shall be
  taken in *their own* naughtiness." (Proverbs 11: 5-6)

  "Better *is* the poor that walketh in his uprightness, than *he
  that is* perverse *in his* ways, though he *be* rich." (Proverbs 28: 6)

  "He that is faithful in that which is least is faithful also in
  much: and he that is unjust in the least is unjust also in
  much." (Luke 16: 10)

  "Finally, brethren, whatsoever things *are* true, whatsoever
  things *are* honest, whatsoever things *are* just, whatsoever
  things *are* pure, whatsoever things *are* lovely, whatsoever

things *are* of good report; if *there be* any virtue, and if *there be* any praise, think on these things." (Philippians 4: 8)

"And as ye would that men should do to you, do ye also to them likewise."   (Luke 6:31)

"And hath not oppressed any *but* hath restored to the debtor his pledge, hath spoiled none by violence, hath given his bread to the hungry, and hath covered the naked with a garment . . . Hath walked in my statutes, and hath kept my judgements, to deal truly; he *is* just, he shall surely live, saith the LORD God." (Ezekiel 18: 7, 9)

"Honour thy father and thy mother: that thy days may be long upon the land which the LORD thy God giveth thee." (Exodus 20: 12)

"*Be* kindly affectioned one to another with brotherly love; in honour preferring one another." (Romans 12: 10)

Reflection(s): "Let it go!" Let nothing and no one get in the way of your march toward greater success, and always remain goal directed and focused on "winning the game". Make sure all the "dots connect" in a rational manner and avoid blockages of progress by others or yourself. In stressful, tense, and emotional situations, time to practice WWWST concepts by using your head, not your mouth until you calm down. Practice: "Let it go!"

Every person at birth starts life with a "good name" and excellent character standing. Such status may be maintained throughout childhood and adulthood or diminished, by choice. To maintain such positive status is simply a matter of doing the right things for the right reasons, not some of the time but all the time. One's honor is defined and enjoyed by self-actions, whether appreciated or not appreciated by others. It is left open to compliments or criticism, but always better to behave with honor and integrity. The idea of speaking and acting honorably is one of the most important choices a person can make, and it can be achieved 100% of the time.

Honor is important in terms of self-reflection and outward appearance. In history those who have been revered for being honorable have consistently demonstrated certain qualities, such as caring for others and for causes bigger than themselves, joy in seeking to help others, honesty, trustworthiness, understanding and an appreciation for loyalty, and comfort in showing love for self and others.

There are far more people in the world who live lives of honor than those who do not. People of honor do not have to announce or define their position. Yet, no one is perfect, and it is possible for a person to take actions on one day which are honorable and on other days to take actions which are not. It should not matter whether another person is watching. People of honor do the right thing whether they are being observed by other people or not.

There are some common terms that clearly define the difference between honorable and dishonorable conduct. For example, honorable people do not cheat; they do not steal; they do not violate the principles of teamwork and act as though they are part of one group and yet take actions of betrayal against the group for their own personal benefit. They take the time to help others any chance they get and are willing to put the greater good in service above themselves. Honorable people are loyal to family, co-workers, teammates, and others. Honorable people are honest, period -- not just some of the time but all the time! And, they mind their own business and do not "mess with other people" for spite or otherwise; they leave other people alone. People of honor know and understand to tell the truth and do the right thing even when doing so may be of some disadvantage to them, personally.

Character traits of honorable people are provided below; some were noted earlier for emphasis. Think of how you and others you know demonstrate the character traits which follow:

- Fair
- Credible
- Concerned about other people and willing to show it
- Positive in relating to others
- Honest
- Full of integrity

- Loyal
- Sensitive, no bullying or teasing of others
- Not discriminatory based upon income levels, class or race
- Trustworthy

I was proud of and thankful for my childhood growth environment for being surrounded by my family, friends, teachers, and church worshippers who were honorable people. The same goes for my adult life. It is a choice I decided to make long ago to surround myself with people of great honor and integrity. At any hint of people being dishonorable, I have always quickly moved away from those people. You can usually tell the difference within minutes, whether people are of honor or not.

I have learned that most people are honorable, hardworking and intend to do good things. We do more toward ensuring a peaceful and friendly environment by showing an attitude of grace and encouragement over discouragement. It is more rewarding for all concerned to believe things can change for the better; I have kept the faith and believe in things hoped for and the evidence of things not yet seen. Practice!

Reader - Think; Share; Reflect: _____

_____

- Honesty - Tell the truth and think, act, and live truthfully in all communications and transactions. Honesty is important whether related to the commission or omission of actions or comments in pursuance of the truth. Even in cases where the truth is not apparent or may be hidden from open view or misunderstood, the best approach is to "fill in the blanks" for accuracy rather than to allow misperceptions or lack of access to truth to prevail. Practice!

  ➢ *Alignment with Bible Passages*:

    "*He that* speaketh truth sheweth forth righteousness: but a false witness deceit." (Proverbs 12:17)

"Lying lips *are* abomination to the LORD: but they that deal truly *are* his delight." (Proverbs 12:22)

"And ye shall know the truth, and the truth shall make you free." (John 8: 32)

"For he that will love life, and see good days, let him refrain his tongue from evil, and his lips that they speak no guile: let him eschew evil, and do good; let him seek peace, and ensue it." (1 Peter 3: 10-11)

"But now ye also put off all these; anger, wrath, malice, blasphemy, filthy communication out of your mouth. Lie not one to another, seeing that ye have put off the old man with his deeds; And have put on the new *man*, which is renewed in knowledge after the image of him that created him." (Colossians 3: 8-10)

"Thou shalt not bear false witness against thy neighbour." (Exodus 20: 16)

"For the wrath of God is revealed from heaven against all ungodliness and unrighteousness of men, who hold truth in unrighteousness." (Romans 1: 18)

"But speak thou the things which become sound doctrine: . . . In all things shewing thyself a pattern of good works: in doctrine *shewing* uncorruptness, gravity, sincerity, Sound speech, that cannot be condemned; that he is of the contrary part may be ashamed, having no evil thing to say of you." (Titus 2: 1, 7-8)

"Let no corrupt communication proceed out of your mouth, but that which is good to the use of edifying, that it may minister grace unto the hearers." (Ephesians 4: 29)

"If any man among you seem to be religious, and bridleth not his tongue, but deceiveth his own heart, this man's religion *is* vain." (James 1: 26)

Reflection(s): "Let it go!" Let nothing and no one get in the way of your march toward greater success, and always remain goal directed and focused on "winning the game". Make sure all the "dots connect" in a rational manner and avoid blockages of progress by others or yourself. In stressful, tense, and emotional situations, time to practice WWWST concepts by using your head, not your mouth until you calm down. Practice: "Let it go!"

It is important to tell the truth, all the time, even when not convenient and when the consequences that follow may feel quite uncomfortable. Everyone prefers to spend time with honest people -- friends or foes. Once a person is exposed as dishonest or lacking in his or her tendencies to be truthful, others will listen differently and cautiously, with hesitation in determining whether to believe what is being communicated. Better to just tell the truth, each time!

Note the following true story about honesty. Carolyn and I traveled through an unfamiliar city late one night in the state of Louisiana, and we were hungry. We stopped at the only fast food restaurant in sight. We bought hamburgers and drinks for a total cost of $16.49. My wife gave the cashier a $20.00 bill, expecting $3.51 in change. The cashier mistakenly gave back $16.49, and my wife attempted to explain that this was the incorrect amount. Thinking that we were lodging a complaint, the cashier did not understand why there was a problem. We showed her the money she had given us, making her realize that she had returned to us the cost of the meal instead of the change amount. Upon understanding her mistake, she thanked us for being honest and said that it had been a long night and she was tired.

By returning the money to the cashier my wife demonstrated honesty and doing the right thing. She made a choice regarding not profiting from someone else's mistake. How would you have handled the situation? Why?

Think about your own stories where you or another person exhibited an honest response or reaction in a situation. Consider, for example, being approached by a person of some authority: a parent, schoolteacher or administrator, police officer, manager of a store or other authority figure. You are thought to have observed a violation of the rules or law, perhaps even an accidental mishap. If approached to serve as a witness to report on what you have observed, what are your thoughts and attitude about how best to approach such a situation?

I was privileged to serve as the first head basketball coach of the current L. C. Anderson High School in Austin, Texas. I can recall vividly a situation where a mistake was made by a referee during a game against the Austin High School team in awarding the ball to the opposing team that should have been awarded to our team. The opposing coach acknowledged the mistake and informed the referee of the mistake simultaneously as our team coaches, players and fans complained. The referee corrected the mistake and awarded the ball to our team but only after the coach of the opposing team spoke. This is a fine demonstration of honesty by the coach, even with the awareness that such honesty would not be beneficial to his team. We won the game, but the opposing coach won a lot of respect for being honest. Practice!

Reader - Think; Share; Reflect: _____

_____

- Listening - To listen is a major component in communication and is as important as speaking. There is a major difference in hearing and listening. Hearing simply perceives the sounds, while listening requires hearing the sounds and applying what is heard to a sense of meaning and determining an appropriate response, if any. Hearing is a natural function of the body in acknowledgement of sound; listening requires thinking and action. Practice!

  ➤ *Alignment with Bible Passages*:

    "Wherefore, my beloved brethren, let every man be swift to hear, slow to speak, slow to wrath." (James 1:19)

"He *is* in the way of life that keepeth instruction: but he that refuseth reproof erreth." (Proverbs 10:17)

"The way of a fool *is* right in his own eyes: but he that hearkeneth unto counsel *is* wise." (Proverbs 12: 15)

"He that answereth a matter before he heareth it, it *is* folly and shame unto him." (Proverbs 18: 13)

"Therefore whatsoever ye have spoken in darkness shall be heard in the light; and that which ye have spoken in the ear in closets shall be proclaimed upon the housetops." (Luke 12: 3)

"Therefore whosoever heareth these sayings of mine, and doeth them, I will liken him unto a wise man, which built his house upon a rock: And the rain descended, and the floods came, and the winds blew, and beat upon that house; and it fell not: for it was founded upon a rock. And every one that heareth these sayings of mine, and doeth them not, shall be likened unto a foolish man, which built his house upon the sand: And the rain descended, and the floods came, and the winds blew, and beat upon that house; and it fell: and great was the fall of it. " (Matthew 7: 24-27)

"But be ye doers of the word, and not hearers only, deceiving your own selves." (James 1: 22)

"But they obeyed not, neither inclined their ear, but made their neck stiff, that they might not hear, nor receive instruction." (Jeremiah 17: 23)

"Call unto me, and I will answer thee, and shew thee great and mighty things, which thou knowest not." (Jeremiah 33: 3)

"Moreover if thy brother shall trespass against thee, go and tell him his fault between thee and him alone: if he shall hear thee, thou hast gained thy brother." (Matthew 18: 15)

Reflection(s): "Let it go!" Let nothing and no one get in the way of your march toward greater success, and always remain goal directed and focused on "winning the game". Make sure all the "dots connect" in a rational manner and avoid blockages of progress by others or yourself. In stressful, tense, and emotional situations, time to practice WWWST concepts by using your head, not your mouth until you calm down. Practice: "Let it go!"

To listen requires thinking and action and not passive hearing of sounds. That is, listening requires making a deliberate attempt to process what is heard and analyzing it for meaning and determination of an appropriate response that is required or expected. It is, therefore, possible for a person to decide to actively not listen, even though the spoken words are heard. Listening requires blocking out of the mind or line of thinking any sounds which may distract from the meaning or intended purpose of the message being delivered.

In my many years of professional life, I have participated in numerous meetings and programs, some as a guest, others requiring attendance as an employee, and some as the host or supervisor -- calling for others to attend. I have worked at and been determined not to allow myself to be distracted during meetings, whether the topic of discussion or discussant was exciting or boring or somewhere in between. I am clear that it is important to listen to every word, whether the conversation is on a personal or professional level -- one or two words in meaning can make a major difference. I believe that much of the knowledge which I have attained has been the result of active listening. Actively listening means to practice the WAPP component, "what to say, when to say it, and when to stop talking". Is it always easy? No, so practice, practice, practice as other winners always do.

Any success I have enjoyed is related to and the result of my listening to others. For example, I listened to my mother, father, teachers, and pastor about the importance of staying in school and succeeding in school from elementary school through earning the doctorate at The

University of Texas at Austin. I listened when my father repeated to me over and over this quote: "You can take a horse to water, but you cannot make him drink". It was a reminder to "let it go" and not push others into something they are not committed to doing. I listened to my high school basketball coaches who told me that I could succeed in college in basketball, prior to my signing a college letter of intent to attend Southwest Texas State University (current name Texas State University) as the first African American athlete. I listened to parents, friends and teachers who instructed classmates and me never to quit something which you enjoy and may bring meaning into your life, saying routinely, "If you believe it, you can achieve it," and "If at first you don't succeed, try, try again." I have listened to my wife and children and enjoyed conversations about the importance of family love and appreciation. I have listened to several physicians about the importance of living a healthy lifestyle and making important choices that enhance quality of life. I have also listened to and benefited from the advice of family, friends, and mentors within and across several groups not to engage in physical fights and not to do drugs. These individuals also helped me gain appreciation for and understanding of the importance of getting along with everyone and to make it a routine practice to reach out to help others. Practice!

Reader - Think; Share; Reflect: _____

_____

- Love (give and seek over hatred) - To love and be loved are equally important and a significant part of enjoying a successful lifestyle. Love, in a real sense, is connected within and across every emotion, thought and action; although, you cannot see it and touch it. It is always there. Each one of us wants to be loved and appreciated, and each one of us has the innate ability to give and receive love. There is no room or good time in a "high quality" lifestyle for hatred, either to spread, devote time to it in thoughts or actions, or to experience it. Practice!

➤ *Alignment with Bible Passages:*

"A new commandment I give unto you, That ye love one another; as I have loved you, that ye also love one another. By this shall all *men* know that ye are my disciples, if ye have love one to another." (John 13: 34-35)

"But the fruit of the Spirit is love, joy, peace, long-suffering, gentleness, goodness, faith, Meekness, temperance: against such there is no law." (Galatians 5:22-23)

"And the second (commandment) *is* like, *namely* this, Thou shalt love thy neighbour as thyself. There is none other commandment greater than these." (Mark 12: 31)

"Ye have heard that it hath been said, Thou shalt love thy neighbour, and hate thine enemy. But I say unto you, Love your enemies, bless them that curse you, do good to them that hate you, and pray for them which despitefully use you, and persecute you; That ye may be the children of your Father which is in heaven: for he maketh his sun to rise on the evil and on the good, and sendeth rain on the just and on the unjust. For if ye love them which love you, what reward have ye? do not even the publicans the same? And if ye salute your brethren only, what do ye more *than others?* do not even the publicans so? Be ye therefore perfect, even as your Father which is in heaven is perfect." (Matthew 5: 43-48)

"*Let* love be without dissimulation. Abhor that which is evil; cleave to that which is good. *Be* kindly affectioned one to another with brotherly love; in honour preferring one another . . . Bless them which persecute you: bless, and curse not. Rejoice with them that do rejoice, and weep with them that weep . . . Recompense to no man evil for evil. Provide things honest in the sight of all men. If it be possible, as much as lieth in you, live peaceably with all men . . . Therefore if thine enemy hunger, feed him; if he thirst, give him drink: for in so doing thou shalt heap coals of fire on his head. Be not overcome of evil, but overcome evil with good." (Romans 12: 9-10; 14-15; 17-18; 20-21)

"Owe no man any thing, but to love one another: for he that loveth another hath fulfilled the law. For this, Thou shalt not commit adultery, Thou shalt not kill, Thou shalt not steal, Thou shalt not bear false witness, Thou shalt not covet; and if *there be* any other commandment, it is briefly comprehended in this saying, namely, Thou shalt love thy neighbour as thyself." (Romans 13: 8-10)

"And let us consider one another to provoke unto love and to good works." (Hebrews 10:24)

"The mouth of a righteous *man is* a well of life: but violence covereth the mouth of the wicked. Hatred stirreth up strifes: but love covereth all sins." (Proverbs 10: 11-12)

"Charity suffereth long, *and* is kind; charity envieth not; charity vaunteth not itself, is not puffed up, Doth not behave itself unseemly, seeketh not her own, is not easily provoked, thinketh no evil; Rejoiceth not in iniquity, but rejoiceth in the truth; Beareth all things, believeth all things, hopeth all things, endureth all things . . . And now abideth faith, hope, charity, these three; but the greatest of these *is* charity." (1 Corinthians 13: 4-7; 13)

"To every *thing there is* a season, and a time to every purpose under the heaven. . . A time to love, and a time to hate; a time of war, and a time of peace. (Ecclesiastes 3: 1; 8)

Reflection(s): "Let it go!" Let nothing and no one get in the way of your march toward greater success, and always remain goal directed and focused on "winning the game". Make sure all the "dots connect" in a rational manner and avoid blockages of progress by others or yourself. In stressful, tense, and emotional situations, time to practice WWWST concepts by using your head, not your mouth until you calm down. Practice: "Let it go!"

I have been fortunate to enjoy true love within and across family, high school and college school classmates, neighbors, church members, and co-workers. Each experience has been grounded in shared, two-way mutual understandings and support. In growing up the love umbrella included my birth family and other relatives: mother and father, sisters and brothers, grandparents, uncles and aunts, and cousins. The love has been strong and unconditional, mutual, and unwavering in the way it has been shared.

The fortune of enjoying true love has continued and grown with the marriage of my wife, Carolyn, and birth, growth and development of our son and two daughters: Berlin Lee Brown, Mary Katherine (Brown) Ruegg and Reesha Johnette (Brown) Edwards and granddaughter, Abigail Sage Ruegg. Each day has been filled with love and affection and support throughout our time together. The in-laws, through marriage, have also been welcoming, supportive and strong in their love and encouragement. One proud example of the love we have all shared is our advocacy for and appreciation of diversity. So, it is no surprise that our youngest daughter attended her high school senior class prom in the company of a diverse group of other students -- via limousine, which our family proudly sponsored. And, no surprise that our family includes bi-racial marriages, and the union of these families together has been very friendly and refreshingly positive.

I can recall many, many examples of expressions of love throughout my life. One example is the time when I left home for college, and my father took what he said was his last money savings he was keeping for dental care and gave it to me for college start-up supplies and well-being. We were economically challenged and, yet, not hungry or experiencing suffering conditions. As a family we always had what we needed, and we counted upon each other for support. My mother was always strong in showing encouragement and unconditional love, even when correcting my brothers, sisters, and me. I sometimes wondered during childhood where she got the energy from, as she would be up early in the morning and late in the evening taking care of the children. She was constantly busy with church and community endeavors in reaching out to help others. She modeled that which she preached, "Take time to help somebody every day". She routinely questioned me and my siblings about what we had done to assist other people and to explain how. She loved her community and church friends and family and showed it up to the date of her death. My father constantly demonstrated love for the family as well. He, too, was always busy working on the job and after work building and refining things at home during my childhood and up to the time of his death. The house lawn was always well-manicured, and flowers and vegetables that he had planted were plentiful. He built a gazebo in our back yard and garage and added a room onto the back of the house, so that we would have more space for our family consisting of him, my mother and six children. Both of my parents were strict about our being successful in school. They understood that the best route for their children to enjoy happiness and well-being as adults was through gaining an excellent education. Carolyn's parents showed the same love and support for Carolyn, her brothers, and sister, according to stories she has shared and my own observations before her parents died. It should be no surprise that Carolyn and I have done our best to show the same love, support, and attention toward our son and two daughters (and granddaughter) throughout their childhood years and to date.

The family reunions on my mother's side of the family occurred routinely, at least once per year and more frequently some years during my childhood and young adult years, primarily in Bryan, Texas, my mother's birthplace. Such gatherings included my mother's parents, sisters and brother and their spouses and my brothers, sisters, and cousins. There was always a lot of food and friendly conversation. Although, there were occasions when it was difficult to pass the test of knowing the name of certain relatives -- that is, responding to the question: "Do you know who I am", time after time, year after year. The reunions would also occur at my home in Austin and, occasionally, in Houston. The love, joy, and caring were always overflowing and genuine. My father did not often travel out of town, so he would not attend except when the reunions were held at our house. I do not recall such reunions with my father's side of the family. Carolyn's family on her father's side also enjoyed reunions during her developing years up to and including several years after our wedding. The family would gather primarily at her home in Paris, Texas and would include family members from West Texas and the state of Oklahoma. It was an occasion which was full of love and caring for one another. I regret that we have not continued such traditions in recent years. Yet, the families within and across my family and Carolyn's were joined for two special occasions, the wedding ceremonies of our daughters, Mary and Reesha. For those two joyous occasions relatives and friends visited from Austin, Dallas, Paris, Houston, and Port Arthur in Texas and from the states of Minnesota, Oregon, Georgia, and Arizona. Our family also enjoyed the pleasure of celebrating together in love and joy at the high school and college graduation ceremonies of Berlin, Mary and Reesha. We had a little more excitement than we had counted upon following Reesha's graduation from college, as the sirens warning of a tornado blasted in the air just as we were leaving the ceremony. Tornadoes did ravage the area of Metro-Atlanta, Georgia but we were all fortunate to avoid injury.

The experiences at Texas State University and The University of Texas were positive from start to finish, throughout my higher education training experiences, whereupon as students we routinely demonstrated love for one another. In both schools I was one of a few African American students in my college programs and classes. The same love and joy held true for my work experiences and faith-based involvement, as the high regard, support and love have been more prevalent than not in interactions among colleagues. I have been fortunate to heed the advice I was given and swift to share with the youth, that is, "hang around those people who will take you up in life" and not around those who will take you down with them. In heeding such advice, I have been fortunate to enjoy success, joy, and loving environments in all phases of life. I happen to believe there is good in each person, and better to look for it than to assume otherwise. At the start as a baby every person begins with the potential to become a loving and pleasant child and adult.

Everyone needs and wants to be loved and appreciated. Yet, not all will admit it, and far too many do not show love in return. I am most fortunate and proud that from birth to present I have enjoyed being part of a loving family. Our family is diverse by race and backgrounds. And our family has routinely been advocates for celebrating diversity and looking at different races and cultures as opportunities to share in experiences and rich dialogue. Practice!

Reader - Think; Share; Reflect: _____

_____

- Loyalty - Loyalty is an important factor for achieving a common goal. Once the members of the group are identified and the group norms are established, there is an expectation of loyalty or agreement with all members of the team or group. Membership will change over time, with new members added and others leaving the group. Once norms are clear and established and there is a goal in mind for winning or high achievement, everyone has to believe in and practice the concept of counting on other members of the group and being counted upon, as a loyal or committed member of the group. Practice!

➤ *Alignment with Bible Passages:*

"A friend loveth at all times, and a brother is born for adversity. A man void of understanding striketh hands, *and* becometh surety in the presence of his friend." (Proverbs 17: 17-18)

"A man *that hath* friends must shew himself friendly: and there is a friend *that* sticketh closer than a brother." (Proverbs 18: 24)

"Most men will proclaim every one his own goodness: but a faithful man who can find?" (Proverbs 20: 6)

"He that followeth after righteousness and mercy findeth life, righteousness and honour." (Proverbs 21: 21)

"Thine own friend, and thy father's friend, forsake not; neither go into thy brother's house in the day of thy calamity:

for better *is* a neighbour *that is* near than a brother far off." (Proverbs 27: 10)

"Greater love hath no man than this, that a man lay down his life for his friends." (John 15:13)

"They went out from us, but they were not of us; for if they had been of us, they would *no doubt* have continued with us: but *they went out*, that they might be made manifest that they were not all of us." (1 John 2: 19)

"Help, LORD; for the godly man ceaseth; for the faithful fail from among the children of men. They speak vanity every one with his neighbour: *with* flattering lips *and* with a double heart do they speak." (Psalm 12: 1-2)

"Let the husband render unto the wife due benevolence: and likewise also the wife unto the husband. The wife hath not power of her own body, but the husband: and likewise also the husband hath not power of his own body, but the wife." (1 Corinthians 7: 3-4)

"*Be* kindly affectioned one to another with brotherly love; in honour preferring one another." (Romans 12: 10)

Reflection(s): "Let it go!" Let nothing and no one get in the way of your march toward greater success, and always remain goal directed and focused on "winning the game". Make sure all the "dots connect" in a rational manner and avoid blockages of progress by others or yourself. In stressful, tense, and emotional situations, time to practice WWWST concepts by using your head, not your mouth until you calm down. Practice: "Let it go!"

Loyalty is a two-way proposition -- you to the team or organization and the team or organization to you. True loyalty is earned on both sides and entails promises and agreements made and kept. Loyalty is not, and should not be, contingent upon nor a mechanism to stifle disagreements. Rather, it should be based upon commonly agreed upon terms, verbal and written, which express mutual benefits for the team or organization and individual. Mutual benefit means that neither the team nor organization acts or is involved in activities that may be harmful or disruptive.

There are clear advantages in the "team" concept, "all for one and one for all" mentality. I have enjoyed actively practicing the "team" approach from as early as childhood and through the "world of work" in employment. Indeed, when the team or organization has a "weak link" in the group, any adverse comments or actions can result in a negative effect and, even, disastrous consequences for all concerned. Consider, for example, the effect of disloyalty and lack of dedication and commitment in an organization such as a circus trapeze act, where one mistake in technique may result in tragedy. Practice leads toward perfection, and not practicing may lead to disaster. And consider a basketball team where a person refuses to practice free throws and the team is faced with an opportunity to win the game with a few seconds left on the clock. Again, practicing leads toward perfection.

I have been most fortunate to participate on athletic teams in high school and college and in employment in associating myself with persons with a strong sense of what it means to be loyal.

If a person is unhappy or disgruntled with the team or organization, it is important to address the matter through established procedures and protocols. Also, never, ever give up when you know you are right, and the facts are on your side and the team or organization is better served by your pursuit of the change you are seeking. Practice!

Reader - Think; Share; Reflect: _____

_____

- Protect property (of self and others and not steal) - It is not complicated. There is no good reason to steal or even think about it. Besides being the wrong thing to do by law and violation in morality, stealing is hurtful to both self and others. It does not matter that no one is around to see you steal; it is just as wrong. At the same time, it is important to plan for and take actions to protect one's own property. Take steps even as simple as keeping keys or wallet in the same, exact place while traveling or sleeping or locking the door behind you for safety and protection of property. Think, plan, practice!

➢ *Alignment with Bible Passages*:

"Thou shalt not steal." (Exodus: 20: 15)

"Let him that stole steal no more: but rather let him labour, working with *his* hands the thing which is good, that he may have to give to him that needeth." (Ephesians 4: 28)

"Thou therefore which teachest another, teachest thou not thyself? thou that preachest a man should not steal, dost thou steal? (Romans 2: 21)

"Lay not up for yourselves treasures upon earth, where moth and rust doth corrupt, and where thieves break through and steal: But lay up for yourselves treasures in heaven, where neither moth nor rust doth corrupt, and where thieves do not break through nor steal: For where your treasure is, there will heart be also." (Matthew 6:19-21)

"My son, if sinners entice thee, consent thou not. If they say, Come with us, let us lay wait for blood, let us lurk privily for the innocent without cause: Let us swallow them up alive as the grave; and whole, as those that go down into the pit: We shall find all precious substance, we shall fill our houses with spoil: Cast in thy lot among us; let us all have one purse: My son, walk not thou in the way with them; refrain thy foot from their path." (Proverbs 1: 10-15)

"And my people shall dwell in a peaceable habitation, and in sure dwellings, and in quiet resting places." (Isaiah 32: 18)

154

"Because thou hast made the LORD, *which is* my refuge, *even* the most high, thy habitation; There shall no evil befall thee, neither shall any plague come nigh thy dwelling. For he shall give his angels charge over thee, to keep thee in all thy ways." (Psalm 91: 9-11)

"When a strong man armed keepeth his palace, his goods are in peace." (Luke 11: 21)

"Again, when I say unto the wicked, Thou shalt surely die; if he turn from his sin, and do that which is lawful and right; *If* the wicked restore the pledge, give again that he had robbed, walk in the statutes of life, without committing iniquity; he shall surely live, he shall not die . . . When the righteous turneth from his righteousness, and committeth iniquity, he shall even die thereby. But if the wicked turn from his wickedness, and do that which is lawful and right, he shall live thereby." (Ezekiel 33: 14-15; 18-19)

"Verily I say unto you, Whosoever shall not receive the kingdom of God as a little child shall in no wise enter therein. And a certain ruler asked him, saying, Good Master, what shall I do to inherit eternal life? And Jesus said unto him, Why callest thou me good? none *is* good, save one, *that is*, God. Thou knowest the commandments, Do not commit adultery, Do not kill, Do not steal, Do not bear false witness, Honour thy father and thy mother." (Luke 18: 17-20)

Reflection(s): "Let it go!" Let nothing and no one get in the way of your march toward greater success, and always remain goal directed and focused on "winning the game". Make sure all the "dots connect" in a rational manner and avoid blockages of progress by others or yourself. In stressful, tense, and emotional situations, time to practice WWWST concepts by using your head, not your mouth until you calm down. Practice: "Let it go!"

I was excited upon earning a "letter jacket" from my high school in recognition of success, following the season of my junior year at the school. About a year later I was not so pleased when the jacket was stolen while friends and I were enjoying time together at the local neighborhood area elementary school. Neither my friends nor I observed the person stealing the jacket. It was out of sight for only a few moments, but I should have been more careful to wear the jacket or maintain sight of it to avoid my property being stolen. The jacket was taken by one of my former classmates and maintained and worn for over 20 years before the person decided to return it through a relative who remained in Austin. The former classmate expressed being overcome by feelings of guilt and decided the way to correct the wrong action was to return the jacket to me through the relative. My family member simply thanked the person for returning the jacket; although, it had an appearance of being old and worn. I was proud of myself and family for demonstrating the ability to "let it go" and move on. I never attempted to identify the person who committed the act of taking the jacket which did not belong to him. I was simply pleased that the jacket was returned to me.

Hurricane Harvey, which occurred during the last few days of August and the start of September 2017, was a true test on the ability to "let it go". The storm drenched Southeast Texas with rain for several days, totaling more measurable inches of rain than over hundreds of years. The storm was a "direct hit" over Port Arthur, Texas, the city in which Carolyn and I reside. Over 80 per cent of homes and businesses in the area were flooded, including our home. The worst day and night of the storm was August 29. The rain poured down all day and night and early the next morning. The storm's effect on us and our property was most challenging, and things got more serious as the storm sewer system broke down, resulting in flooding of homes and businesses throughout the city.

We made attempts to protect our home from flooding through what we thought were common sense actions, such as stacking towels and "throw rugs" at each house entrance -- front and back doors and garage door. We even made attempts to cover the bottom of tables and chairs with plastic bags to prevent water damage. Such actions were no match for "mother nature". Our efforts were no match for the water rising inside our house. By the end of the day, August 29, we observed that in spite of our intense efforts to protect our property, water began to seep through cracks in and around the doors, walls and foundation of the house; we had lost our battle with the storm for sure at approximately 7:00 p.m. The carpet on the floors in our master and other bedrooms filled quickly with water at that point. The water in the garage rose quickly as well. Our pet Chihuahua showed signs of panic -- like the panic that he must have observed in the faces of Carolyn and me.

The time had come to gather the essentials and move to the upstairs area of the house. Fortunately, we had that as an option. The time had come to "let it go" for now and focus on survival and deal with the property interests later. The neighbors next door and we communicated several times throughout the night. For example, we talked about issues such as the need to ensure the electrical breakers were turned off as soon as possible. The house construction contractor -- who lives in the neighborhood -- alerted us to be sure that in order to prevent electrical shock, we should wear rubber boots or some type of foot covering in the house prior to attempting to turn off the breakers.

If one were to raise the questions of how serious the situation was and why we and others did not leave prior to the flooding, the answers may be easily given: a. How serious? The flooding was so bad we had to depart in a boat; b. Why not leave earlier? The water rose very quickly, and conditions worsened beyond what was anticipated due to the amount of rain and the sewage drainage system broke down in the middle of the storm. Roads and highways were flooded and closed for many miles, leaving automobiles inoperable. Hotels were flooded as well. The Civic Center which was opened as a local shelter was also flooded to the point that those who sought shelter there were required to sit in the bleachers.

We were fortunate that our neighbor contacted friends who own a boat and were most generous with their time and efforts to lift several neighbors, my wife and me out of harm's way. The street flooding was so bad that the water sat in the streets a couple of weeks in some areas, making travel on those streets impassable. We were also fortunate to gain access to a local church shelter for an overnight stay, and we gained access to one of the few available hotel rooms for the following night. We remained in various local hotels for about four months, sponsored by the

United States Government – Federal Emergency Management Agency (FEMA) for which we are eternally grateful. Such support came only after numerous phone calls and emails, however. FEMA also provided temporary shelter in the form of a trailer which was placed on our home property for several months, pending completion of repairs to our home. We were quite privileged to enjoy such an opportunity, which enabled us to be in a better position to protect our property and enable us to curtail our stint of living in hotels; we were more than ready to go home by this point. Regrettably, the management in some of the hotels implemented regulations that restricted room availability to cash paying customers only and, thereby, blocking access to those potential customers who were sponsored by FEMA. Such a practice wreaked of unfair housing discrimination intended to accept for housing only affluent customers, thereby, blocking access to most of Southeast Texas residents.

The transition from the flood, staying in hotels and living in the trailer took over a year and a half before we were able to move back into our home. The work from "gutting" the house of carpet, walls, tile floors and furniture, followed by the required renovation work and replacement of appliances and furniture took a lot of patience and money. We were fortunate to have flood and windstorm insurance, for sure. And by living in a somewhat rural area, the trustworthy contractors were limited in number. We kept the faith – in things hoped for and the evidence of things not yet seen. Practice!

Reader - Think; Share; Reflect: _____

_____

- Reading - Reading is basic to all other knowledge, and it is key to all learning and the "spine" which holds everything together. If you cannot read, everybody will know it. Also, there is no "victory" in being illiterate. When you speak, your speech is a clear and public indicator of your level of preparation and intelligence. Reading is a means to acquire communication skills. A person who is a poor or reluctant reader shows his or her lack of preparation and obvious unwillingness to grow in the skill set required for a good fit in society. You have a choice whether to be viewed as intelligent or unintelligent and, like any other skill set, you must practice each day to improve. Practice!

➤ *Alignment with Bible Passages*:

"The fear of the LORD *is* the beginning of knowledge: *but* fools despise wisdom and instruction. My son, hear the instruction of thy father, and forsake not the law of thy mother. For they *shall* be an ornament of grace unto thy head, and chains about thy neck." (Proverbs 1: 7-9)

"Wisdom *is* the principal thing; *therefore* get wisdom: and with all thy getting get understanding." (Proverbs 4:7)

"Every wise woman buildeth her house: but the foolish plucketh it down with her hands. . .The wisdom of the prudent *is* to understand his way: but the folly of fools *is* deceit." (Proverbs 14: 1; 8)

"The heart of him that hath understanding seeketh knowledge: but the mouth of fools feedeth on foolishness." (Proverbs 15:14)

"The wise in heart shall be called prudent: and the sweetness of the lips increaseth learning. Understanding *is* a wellspring of life unto him that hath it: but the instruction of fools *is* folly. The heart of the wise teacheth his mouth, and addeth learning to his lips. Pleasant words *are as* an honeycomb, sweet to the soul, and health to the bones." (Proverbs 16: 21-24)

"Day unto day uttereth speech, and night unto night sheweth knowledge." (Psalm 19: 2)

"Teach me good judgment and knowledge: for I have believed thy commandments." (Psalm 119: 66)

"Therefore whosoever heareth these sayings of mine, and doeth them, I will liken him unto a wise man, which built his house upon a rock: And the rain descended, and the floods came, and the winds blew, and beat upon that house; and it fell not: for it was founded upon a rock. And everyone that heareth these sayings of mine, and doeth them not, shall be likened unto a foolish man, which built his house upon the sand: And the rain descended, and the floods came, and the winds blew, and beat upon that house; and it fell: and great was the fall of it." (Matthew 7: 24-27)

"For wisdom *is* a defence, *and* money is a defence: but the excellency of knowledge is, *that* wisdom giveth life to them that have it." (Ecclesiastes 7: 12)

"For whatsoever things were written aforetime were written for our learning, that we through patience and comfort of the scriptures might have hope." (Romans 15: 4)

Reflection(s): "Let it go"! Let nothing and no one get in the way of your march toward greater success, and always remain goal directed and focused on "winning the game". Make sure all the "dots connect" in a rational manner and avoid blockages of progress by others or yourself. In stressful, tense, and emotional situations, time to practice WWWST concepts by using your head, not your mouth until you calm down. Practice: "Let it go"!

Reading is especially important! Read; read; read and read even more -- never enough! Reading is one of the most important skill sets imaginable. It is so important because reading is a requirement for all aspects of intelligence, knowledge, and communication. It is a fact that when you read, you grow in knowledge and skills through practice.

I read each day and have done so for many, many years; the same goes for Carolyn. I was fortunate to enjoy the experience as a first and second grade student, with Mrs. Poole and Mrs. Harris, who, along with my parents and siblings, ensured that my classmates and I were taught how and encouraged to read. Other teachers beyond second grade also did an excellent job in assuring the conditions were favorable for student success in reading. We learned early in life how important reading is in leading toward a happy, high quality lifestyle, and my parents and educators were right. Our lessons were consistent in substance, and teachers insisted that students practice at home. The terms were not necessarily announced during my early years why we practiced various aspects of our learning how to read successfully. However, as I advanced educationally and professionally, the need to possess good reading skills became quite clear. In reviewing current research and practice, the approach utilized by teachers was primarily consistent and aligned with basic understandings on how best to teach children how to read, including the following:

- Building phonemic awareness or sound segmentation strategies.
- Learning phonics and decoding of words.
- Practicing reading fluency and automatic recognition of words in text.
- Practicing vocabulary skills and increasing vocabulary banks over time.
- Comprehension of text while reading.
- Expression through writing.
- Connecting reading and writing to complement each other in increasing overall literacy.
- Emphasizing spelling, more at that time than currently; and
- Practicing handwriting skills, again, more at that time than currently.

Upon becoming an educator, I was truly clear about the importance of all teachers encouraging children to read frequently and with fluency and strong comprehension. During the time of my experience as sports coach: football, basketball, track, tennis and swimming at the middle school level, and football and basketball at the high school level, I encouraged our athletes to read. Texas now has state laws about student athletes being required to "pass" to "play" or performing successfully in classes to participate in sports. As a coach I implemented rules for passing to play long before the state-imposed legislation for participation.

"No pass-No play" under my direction as coach went beyond the low-level expectation of passing. My rule as high school coach was that team members should make "A"s and "B"s in classes or face consequences. We established a culture of excellence where we expected our athletes to succeed, and they agreed through their actions and reports of success.

We took the time each grading period to highlight the results of our hard work for excellent achievement in academics. I also required the athletes to stay out of trouble in school and beyond. And we established a culture of excellence and championship behavior as the norm. We enjoyed victories in the classroom and in winning games on the basketball court. As high school basketball coach at the L.C. Anderson High School in Austin, our record for our best year of performance was: 24 wins and six losses, including only one loss in district play. I was honored to be selected as the Coach of the Year for that season. In our final game that year, we lost a "nail-biter" to John H. Reagan High School of Austin during a bi-district playoff game at Gregory Gymnasium at The University of Texas at Austin. We played the game in a larger gymnasium than our ordinary high school site due to the anticipated size of the audience. I considered our players to be champions in the classroom and as competitive athletes. We routinely emphasized reading before, during, and after the school days.

In determining what to read as an adult, I make deliberate efforts to mix it up every day: magazines; newspapers -- at least two to three per day; internet surfing; fiction and non-fiction novels; Bible; and professional literature. I find it to be refreshing and fun to spend time writing every chance I get, which is most days. I am proud to be part of a family of readers: from my birth family, including mother and father; sisters and brothers; and, wife, Carolyn; and our son and two daughters and sons-in-law, each of whom graduated from college. Practice matters!

Reader - Think; Share; Reflect: _____

_____

- Respect (self and others and mind your business) - You deserve to be respected and so does everyone else. Respect starts with self and how you think and act and is apparent in all you say and do. It is far better to demonstrate positive regard toward others than to leave interpretation of your intent to chance. It is also important to give and receive respectful gestures and non-verbal cues in communication with other people. When confronted with decisions on whether to get involved or not, better to mind your own business, especially if the issue is not of your direct concern. Stay out of it. Practice!

➢ *Alignment with Bible Passages*:

Golden Rule: "Therefore all things whatsoever ye would that men should do to you, do ye even so to them: for this is the law and the prophets." (Matthew 7: 12)

"*Let* love be without dissimulation. Abhor that which is evil; cleave to that which is good. *Be* kindy affectioned one to another with brotherly love; in honour preferring one another." (Romans 12: 9-10)

"*Let* nothing *be done* through strife or vainglory; but in lowliness of mind let each esteem other better than themselves." (Philippians 2:3)

"Honour all *men*. Love the brotherhood. Fear God. Honour the king." (1 Peter 2:17)

"Even as I please all *men* in all *things*, not seeking mine own profit, but the *profit* of many, that they may be saved." (1 Corinthians 10: 33)

"For we dare not make ourselves of the number, or compare ourselves with some that commend themselves: but they measuring themselves by themselves, and comparing themselves among themselves, are not wise." (2 Corinthians 10: 12)

"A new commandment I give unto you, That ye love one another; as I have loved you, that ye also love one another. By this shall all *men* know that ye are my disciples, if ye have love one to another." (John 13: 34-35)

"He that oppresseth the poor reproacheth *his* Maker: but he that honoureth him hath mercy on the poor . . . Whoso mocketh the poor reproacheth *his* Maker: *and* he that is glad at calamities shall not be unpunished." (Proverbs 14: 31; 17: 5)

"In all things *shewing* thyself a pattern of good works: in doctrine *shewing* uncorruptness, gravity, sincerity, Sound speech, that cannot be condemned; that he that is of the contrary part may be ashamed, having no evil thing to say of you. . . For the grace of God that bringeth salvation hath appeared to all men, Teaching us that, denying ungodliness and worldly lusts, we should live soberly, righteously, and godly, in this present world." (Titus 2: 7-8; 11-12)

"And we beseech you, brethren, to know them which labour among you, and are over you in the LORD, and admonish you; And to esteem them very highly in love for their work's sake. *And* be at peace among yourselves." (1 Thessalonians 5: 12-13)

Reflection(s): "Let it go!" Let nothing and no one get in the way of your march toward greater success, and always remain goal directed and focused on "winning the game". Make sure all the "dots connect" in a rational manner and avoid blockages of progress by others or yourself. In stressful, tense, and emotional situations, time to practice WWWST concepts by using your head, not your mouth until you calm down. Practice: "Let it go!"

The idea of respecting oneself and others goes beyond words and direct actions. It is also a reflection and demonstration of one's attitude as demonstrated in verbal and non-verbal communication. There is much that can be accomplished, and progress made in communication, if only we look beyond our personal ideas on what a person should look or act like. People, whether intentionally or unintentionally, decide or make attempts to control what others say and do. Respecting another person should not depend upon whether that person follows the same approach as others may wish or think appropriate. In thinking like a champion, we should all work at <u>leaving other people alone</u> and looking for ways to understand and support each other instead of dictating or criticizing. And always, always respect yourself.

Among other measures of strength and maturity of people in business, sports and entertainment is the show of comfort in acknowledging and applauding someone else for excellence in performance -- especially when they perform better at some skill or project than you. It takes a confident person to admit someone else is better at something, even if just momentarily. On the other hand, it is "small" and overly competitive to know it and not acknowledge it. If you consider the definition of average, it is not possible for everyone or everything to be above average. Rather than sulk or complain that someone is better than you at something, it is better to praise the good and strive to improve, moving toward the level of performance or skill set that you admire in someone else. Be excited for your colleagues when they accomplish something special and let them know it.

I was fortunate to grow up in an environment where the family members respected one another, and the same held true among my teachers and classmates, church members and neighborhood. The respect spanned within and across all aspects of the Emerson Street environment. Did we have disagreements among these groups? Yes, but we made deliberate attempts to agree or disagree, while demonstrating respect throughout our communication opportunities. We expressed ourselves by sharing thoughts on situations. There was no abuse, insults, "put downs", or any kind of attack on each other as individuals.

During my elementary and secondary school experiences, the classmates routinely showed respect for one another. The love and appreciation continued up to and including today among my classmates that I grew up with in Austin, Texas. We were able to avoid distinctions on how one of us would be treated or respected based upon financial standing or whether a person was an athlete or in the band or other clubs or extracurricular affiliations. We were proud and respectful of all of those in our company as youth, and that has continued throughout adulthood. Each month our high school classmates gather to communicate on the telephone for a prayer session. We take the time to share prayers and thoughts of wisdom which each one of us may wish to share. The conversations are always respectful and caring, and we have never shared a negative comment about anyone.

I have incredibly positive thoughts and memories about my work environments. I have been fortunate to be surrounded by others whose professionalism and attitudes have been consistent with mine. Terms like excuse me, thank you, would you mind, I appreciate you and your contributions and please have been used commonly among colleagues throughout my interactions in the work environment. It has not been unusual for my colleagues to spend time at lunch or dinner inside and outside the office and issuing invitations for enjoying home meals together. Caution -- be careful in leadership not to require employees to eat during a multi-hour meeting, where food is brought in to save time, thereby, denying employees the break time away from the duties of the day. In my experience as employee, some of the most pleasant gatherings occurred during those break times where colleagues and I would leave the office building and enjoy lunch together outside of the office setting.

It is particularly important that each one of us shows respect for ourselves if we expect or want other people to show respect for us. Additionally, each one of us should make it a priority to show respect for other people. And always keep in mind the thought: <u>leave other people alone</u>! Respect may be earned, but it is not ever given as the result of intimidation or based upon fear, demands or threats of harm. Practice!

Reader - Think; Share; Reflect: _____

_____

- Right way (over wrong) - It is not complicated. Do the right thing, regardless of the circumstances or what may appear to be a possible advantage to do otherwise. Doing the right thing enables you to enjoy the available benefits, while doing the wrong thing works in the opposite direction, short or long term. The decision to do right or wrong starts internally. If you must think about it, whether the action is right or wrong, always, always choose to do the "right" thing over wrong. The self-monitoring mechanisms inside should guide you in the right direction, with heavy reliance upon past experiences and an internal knowledge base in place to guide you. Practice!

➢ *Alignment with Bible Passages*:

"Therefore to him that knoweth to do good, and doeth *it* not, to him it is sin." (James 4: 17)

"For we know that the law is spiritual: but I am carnal, sold under sin. For that which I do I allow not: for what I would, that do I not; but what I hate, that do I. If then I do that which I would not, I consent unto the law that it *is* good. Now then it is no more I that do it, but sin that dwelleth in me . . . For the good that I would I do not: but the evil which I would not, that I do." (Romans 7: 14-17; 19)

"Be not overcome of evil, but overcome evil with good." (Romans 12: 21)

"Blessed *are* the peacemakers: for they shall be called the children of God. Blessed *are* they which are persecuted for righteousness' sake: for theirs is the kingdom of heaven. Blessed are ye, when *men* shall revile you, and persecute *you*, and shall say all manner of evil against you, falsely, for my sake. Rejoice, and be exceeding glad: for great is your reward in heaven: for so persecuted they the prophets which were before you." (Matthew 5: 9-12)

"Envyings, murders, drunkenness, revellings, and such like: of the which I tell you before, as I have also told *you* in time past, that they which do such things shall not inherit the kingdom of God. But the fruit of the Spirit is love, joy, peace, long-suffering, gentleness, goodness, faith, Meekness, temperance: against such there is no law." (Galatians 5: 21-23)

"Little children, let no man deceive you: he that doeth righteousness is righteous, even as he is righteous." (1 John 3: 7)

"For, brethren, ye have been called unto liberty; only *use* not liberty for an occasion to the flesh, but by love serve one another. For all the law is fulfilled in one word, *even* in this; Thou shalt love thy neighbour as thyself. But if ye bite and devour one another, take heed that ye be not consumed one of another." (Galatians 5: 13-15)

"And let us not be weary in well doing: for in due season we shall reap, if we faint not. As we have therefore opportunity, let us do good unto all *men*, especially unto them who are of the household of faith." (Galatians 6: 9-10)

"After this manner therefore pray ye: Our Father which art in heaven, Hallowed be thy name. Thy kingdom come. Thy will be done in earth, *as it is* in heaven. Give us this day our daily bread. And forgive us our debts, as we forgive our debtors. And lead us not into temptation, but deliver us from evil: For thine is the kingdom, and the power, and the glory, forever. Amen. For if ye forgive men their trespasses, your heavenly Father will also forgive you: But if ye forgive not men their trespasses, neither will your Father forgive your trespasses." (Matthew 6: 9-15)

"Be ye strong therefore, and let not your hands be weak: for your work shall be rewarded." (2 Chronicles 15: 7)

Reflection(s): "Let it go!" Let nothing and no one get in the way of your march toward greater success, and always remain goal directed and focused on "winning the game". Make sure all the "dots connect" in a rational manner and avoid blockages of progress by others or yourself.

In stressful, tense, and emotional situations, time to practice WWWST concepts by using your head, not your mouth until you calm down. Practice: "Let it go!"

In life there will be times when you are faced with challenges for determining right from wrong in personal and professional environments. Even when others may encourage you to do the wrong thing, it is always better to choose right over wrong. This is especially important when the decisions are associated with moral, ethical, and legal issues. Examples are: contract management; personnel actions; financial considerations; speed-limit driving; drugs; bullying or bothering people; no stealing.

Think about it in terms of consequences people face after an action is taken or in absence of a person doing the right thing -- consider risk-reward terms. You can count on it that someone else will know or find out about the situation and will tell someone else. It is a regular, normal occurrence that people want to talk, especially about those instances when they know of someone doing the wrong thing. It is always better when faced with decisions to do that which is right, period.

It is not just a matter of being practical. It is a matter of being careful, smart, and wise. You stand a much better chance of "winning the game" in sports and life when you follow the rules and do things the right way. You should, therefore, always consider what will happen when you operate out of bounds or contrary to what is right. You face being singled out by the game officials if involved in a sports activity and by law or work officials in cases of a law or policy violation. What follows then are consequences along with shame and humiliation, often, in public or social media reports.

I can vividly recall a situation where high school teachers in a central Texas school planned a science class field trip where the students would learn about nature during a river boat ride. Some students who happened to be cheerleaders and athletes participated in sneaking alcohol onto the boat and drinking during the boat ride. They were caught as one of the teachers observed empty beer cans being thrown into the water. The teachers reported the incident to school officials after the trip, and all students faced punishment following the trip. The punishment was strong, as a preventative measure and to demonstrate that even cheerleaders and athletes would face serious consequences for such violations. There were a lot of discussions among parents of the students, central office and campus officials and community leaders, in disagreement about whether the punishments were fair or excessive. All of this could have been avoided if only the students had done the right thing in the first place. Regrettably, one of the contributing factors which led to the debate was that the students involved were active and popular students. Again, do the right thing and avoid such drama. Practice!

Reader - Think; Share; Reflect: _____

_____

- Space (give, protect, stay in your lane) - It is most difficult to accurately determine whether someone wants or does not want a person in their "space" or near them. Better to "play it safe" and always be mindful that personal space is deserved by everyone, and a violation of that privilege can often cause discomfort for them and you. Make sure you are "invited" in proximity, with no exceptions of leaving it to chance or guessing, if okay. If not sure of an invitation into another person's "space", keep a safe distance away from him or her. On the other hand, if you believe your private space is being violated, quietly move away to create a greater distance away from you, or simply inform the other person of your feeling of discomfort. Practice!

- ➤ *Alignment with Bible Passages:*

  "The lines are fallen unto me in pleasant *places*; yea, I have a goodly heritage . . . I have set the LORD always before me: because *he is* at my right hand, I shall not be moved." (Psalm 16: 6; 8)

  "With all lowliness and meekness, with long-suffering, forbearing one another in love; Endeavouring to keep the unity of the Spirit in the bond of peace." (Ephesians 4: 2-3)

"Let no corrupt communication proceed out of your mouth, but that which is good to the use of edifying, that it may minister grace unto the hearers." (Ephesians 4: 29)

"Finally, *be ye* all of one mind, having compassion one of another, love as brethren, *be* pitiful, *be* courteous: Not rendering evil for evil, or railing for railing: but contrariwise blessing; knowing that ye are thereunto called, that ye should inherit a blessing. For he that will love life, and see good days, let him refrain his tongue from evil, and his lips that they speak no guile: let him eschew evil, and do good; let him seek peace, and ensue it." (1 Peter 3: 8-11)

"To every *thing there is* a season, and a time to every purpose under the heaven: A time to be born, and a time to die; a time to plant, and a time to pluck up *that which* is planted; A time to kill, and a time to heal; a time to break down, and a time to build up; A time to weep, and a time to laugh; a time to mourn, and a time to dance; A time to cast away stones, and a time to gather stones together; a time to embrace, and a time to refrain from embracing; A time to get, and a time to lose; a time to keep, and a time to cast away; A time to rend, and a time to sew; a time to keep silence, and time to speak; A time to love, and a time to hate; a time of war, and a time of peace." (Ecclesiastes 3: 1-8)

"*Let your* conversation *be* without covetousness; *and be* content with such things as ye have: for he hath said, I will never leave thee, nor forsake thee. So that we may boldly say, The LORD is my helper, and I will not fear what man shall do unto me." (Hebrews 13: 5-6)

"Beware lest any man spoil you through philosophy and vain deceit, after the tradition of men, after the rudiments of the world, and not after Christ." (Colossians 2: 8)

"Ye have heard that it hath been said, Thou shalt love thy neighbour, and hate thine enemy. But I say unto you, Love your enemies, bless them that curse you, do good to them that hate you, and pray for them which despitefully use you, and persecute you." (Matthew 5: 43-44)

"And the King shall answer and say unto them, Verily I say unto you, Inasmuch as ye have done *it* unto one of the least of these my brethren, ye have done *it* unto me . . . Then shall he answer them, saying, Verily I say unto you, Inasmuch as ye did *it* not to one of the least of these, ye did *it* not to me." (Matthew 25: 40; 45)

"Owe no man any thing, but to love one another: for he that loveth another hath fulfilled the law. For this, Thou shalt not commit adultery, Thou shalt not kill, Thou shalt not steal, Thou shalt not bear false witness, Thou shalt not covet; *and if there be* any other commandment, it *is* briefly comprehended in this saying, namely, Thou shalt love thy neighbour as thyself. Love worketh no ill to his neighbour: therefore love *is* the fulfilling of the law." (Romans 13: 8-10)

Reflection(s): "Let it go!" Let nothing and no one get in the way of your march toward greater success, and always remain goal directed and focused on "winning the game". Make sure all the "dots connect" in a rational manner and avoid blockages of progress by others or yourself. In stressful, tense, and emotional situations, time to practice "stop talking" concepts by using your head, not your mouth until you calm down. Practice: "Let it go!"

The idea that there are times when a person just wants to be left alone is not a foreign or unique concept. It is a sense of reality which all of us wish to enjoy, some more often or less than others. There is a commonly accepted phrase, "Don't just do something, sit", or "Don't keep talking, be quiet – or stop talking". It is not just okay to be left alone, I believe it is a very natural experience. Whether the time is spent in reading, watching television or an activity or just taking time to relax or think, we all deserve and should take the time to enjoy our "space" without interruption. Therefore, it is also imperative that when it is not clear that your company is desired, let it go and move away.

Think of those times when a person may wish to dine alone. It is not unusual for another person to approach the person who is dining and make an offer to sit with him or her for the meal. They may approach the person and state, "I hate to see you sitting there eating alone". Guess what? There are times when a person wants and needs to enjoy the "space" and be left alone. The person who is alone should not be pressured to explain or be required to state a reason for the preference to be left to dine alone at that time.

I happen to be one of those who sometimes enjoys eating alone or with family. There are also times when I am comfortable with sharing mealtime with friends and associates. I can recount numerous times when someone approached me at work with an offer to take me out for dinner or lunch, at their cost. I have declined to accept those offers most of the time because such generosities result in an unwelcomed extension of the workday with the effect of taking away the time and opportunities for my preferred routine of eating alone or with family. Of course, I am always appreciative of genuine offers of hospitality. I believe it is important to protect my "space" relative to the time dedicated to personal preferences such as my own dining routines and those times dedicated for reading, meditation and thinking.

How about other times, such as while shopping, or walking in the park or taking time to attend a program or watch a movie at the theatre or the idea of wanting to spend some "me" or "self" time at home? It should be left to the individual to determine whether to enjoy the time or space alone or with company. When a person indicates he or she wishes to be left alone is not time to automatically decide their state of mind or whether there is a problem. There are many times when I just want to meditate or enjoy the time alone and not be interrupted or bothered by another person. In those instances, I would rather not talk on the telephone or engage in conversation with others. Of course, family is more special and always welcomed.

Think about why there is conflict when a person is offended – the individual wants to be left alone or is upset because he believes he is being disrespected. We should avoid making attempts to control another person through our words or actions. Concomitantly, we should not allow ourselves to become offended just because another person wishes to enjoy their space alone or in the company of others outside ourselves. Many conflicts may be avoided if we just follow a simple rule: "Better to 'play it safe' and be mindful that personal space is deserved by everyone." And, again, in thinking like a champion, we should all work at <u>leaving other people alone</u>! Practice!

Reader - Think; Share; Reflect: _____

_____

- Teamwork (over self) - The concept of placing team or common good over self is one of the most cherished notions across the world. It is what is being practiced when, as a nation or church group or athletic team or any similar organization, the preferred standard is what is good for one is good for all. It has been said that "you cannot be almost on the team". You are on the team and act as such, or you are not really a full member of the group. Placing team over self is one of the most important principles of team sports and winning the game. It is also part of what drives the laws we live by and other rules which govern the common good. Practice!

  ➤ *Alignment with Bible Passages*:

    "Two *are* better than one; because they have a good reward for their labour. For if they fall, the one will lift up his fellow: but woe to him *that is* alone when he falleth; for *he hath* not another to help him up. Again, if two lie together, then they have heat: but how can one be warm *alone*? And if one prevail against him, two shall withstand him; and a threefold cord is not quickly broken." (Ecclesiastes 4: 9-12)

    "Now I beseech you, brethren, by the name of our Lord Jesus Christ, that ye all speak the same thing, and *that* there be no divisions among you; but *that* ye be perfectly joined together in the same mind and in the same judgment." (1 Corinthians 1: 10)

"And let us consider one another to provoke unto love and to good works: Not forsaking the assembling of ourselves together, as the manner of some *is*; but exhorting *one another*: and so much the more, as ye see the day approaching." (Hebrews 10: 24-25)

"BEHOLD, how good and how pleasant *it is* for brethren to dwell together in unity!" (Psalm 133:1)

"For as we have many members in one body, and all members have not the same office: So we *being* many, are one body in Christ, and every one members one of another." (Romans 12: 4-5)

"*Be* kindly affectioned one to another with brotherly love; in honour preferring one another." (Romans 12: 10)

"We then that are strong ought to bear the infirmities of the weak, and not to please ourselves. Let every one of us please *his* neighbour for *his* good to edification." (Romans 15: 1-2)

"Iron sharpeneth iron; so a man sharpeneth the countenance of his friend." (Proverbs 27: 17)

"*Let* nothing *be done* through strife or vainglory; but in lowliness of mind let each esteem other better than themselves. Look not every man on his own things, but every man also on the things of others." (Philippians 2: 3-4)

"And let us consider one another to provoke unto love and to good works: Not forsaking the assembling of ourselves together, as the manner of some *is*; but exhorting *one another*:

and so much the more, as ye see the day approaching."
(Hebrews 10: 24-25)

Reflection(s): "Let it go!" Let nothing and no one get in the way of your march toward greater success, and always remain goal directed and focused on "winning the game". Make sure all the "dots connect" in a rational manner and avoid blockages of progress by others or yourself. In stressful, tense, and emotional situations, time to practice WWWST concepts by using your head, not your mouth until you calm down. Practice: "Let it go!"

Successful teams consistently demonstrate characteristics which are observable and well-practiced, where the concept of team is emphasized above self. Among other important strategies to achieve team success, it is critical to "connect the dots" in planning and in all phases of practicing and operating on a system approach, recognizing that all parts are interrelated. This concept is important for all teams: ballet, circus, sports teams, fine arts units, card players, family units, all other teams, and businesses. If, for example, practice is to start at 3:00 p.m., everyone on the team must arrive prior to 3:00 p.m. When the coach calls a play for the team to run during practice or a game, each person is responsible to do what is expected and to do it with great passion and effort. The president of an organization gives a directive to employees on how a report is to be written. When the report is completed and turned in, it should reflect what was directed. In an "own the store" mentality in business operations or school system, each person associated with the company should perform at the best of his or her talents and with a sense of strong "team" concept, realizing the product produced or outcomes can be only as good as the weakest link of workers' accomplishments.

While playing on the L. C. Anderson High School basketball team, we shouted a slogan prior to each game: "All for One – One for All!" We said those words loudly and with joy and commitment and meaning that we were proud members of the team and planned to operate as one. With those words we were acknowledging that what affects one of us affects all of us. We were also proclaiming that each one of us was committing our word to contributing as individuals in support of the team to win the game. Consider any team which is comprised of numerous "super" talented individuals, but they do not perform as champion teammates -- good, but not great. One quite common factor in such a situation is the lack of commitment to each other, and one or more members of the group tends to insist on placing his or her interests above that of the team.

The team concept naturally aligns with groups other than athletic teams. For example, consider work related organizations and departments, church groups, boy scouts and girl scouts' organizations, school clubs and more. The excellent teammates go beyond the words and practice and take actions that when the team is involved, it is not ever about "me", or "I", it is about what is best for the team. Consider the work that goes into becoming an excellent marching band, for example. It is not unusual for selection to be competitive and hard work just to make the team. What follows is practice for hours and hours on playing the music and learning the routines and coordinating the steps and patterns where each performer is on cue in playing the music and marching steps required. No excuses are acceptable, and during the live performances everyone who is present in the audience observes the level of excellence with joy, celebration, and approval or disappointment. The performance is accepted by the performers and audience only when and if the music is good and routines are well coordinated by all members of the band -- teamwork!

Winning is fun and losing is not. Excellent teams and businesses routinely enjoy an environment where each person in the organization is treated with respect and dignity, and they are made to feel valued. They enjoy their work and being part of something special. Consider successful championship teams, such as in college football, University of Alabama, Clemson University, and more recently, Louisiana State University (LSU). The coaches and players work hard at their craft, and they pay special, laser focus attention to details. They also make commitments to each other that they will execute their responsibility each play while on the playing field. And they have fun. For example, I recall observing the excitement among Alabama football players during a practice meeting when superstar national basketball player, Kobe Bryant (now deceased) visited and gave tips on thinking and acting like champions. I also observed several times following victories the Clemson

University players and coaches enjoying dancing the "electric slide" in the dressing room -- well-coordinated and fun! The schools provide the resources and overall conditions for success, as demonstrated at LSU through the completion of the multi-million-dollar locker room, which includes sleep pods, a pool, and a mini theater. The ideas of hard work and enjoyment are interjected into their programs and promoted in all communications among players, coaches, and other personnel.

Sometimes in leadership the simplest gestures can help with team building. For example, I can recall the enthusiasm when as principal at a middle school, I asked what would make the environment more pleasing, and the answer from the employees was they preferred brand-named toilet tissue. Asked and answered immediately by replacing the stock, system product with brand named products, specifically the brands preferred by the employees. In a similar move as superintendent in two separate school districts, I asked the employees their opinions on what would help to improve the work environment and strengthen morale, and the answer was they preferred the school calendar allow for a full week off duty during the Thanksgiving Holidays --asked-answered! "Teamwork makes the dream work" is activated in live form and reality when those who are associated with team believe they are part of something special, they feel empowered and appreciated, and they are inspired beyond the words to do good for the team by what they see in the efforts of the leaders and each of their teammates. Practice!

Reader - Think; Share; Reflect: _____

_____

- Trustworthiness (trust, trusted) - The principle of trustworthiness is simple to understand but difficult for some to follow, either to trust or be trusted. When a person shares information or receives it, better that it remains among those who are directly engaged in the communication, written or verbal form. Whether the communication occurs among those in a small group of two or many more, it is important to practice the skills for trusting and being trustworthy.

➢ *Alignment with Bible Passages*:

"What shall we then say to these things? If God *be* for us, who *can be* against us? He that spared not his own Son, but delivered him up for us all, how shall he not with him also freely give us all things." (Romans 8: 31-32)

"In all things shewing thyself a pattern of good works: in doctrine *shewing* uncorruptness, gravity, sincerity, Sound speech, that cannot be condemned; that he that is of the contrary part may be ashamed, having no evil thing to say of you. . . For the grace of God that bringeth salvation hath appeared to all men, Teaching us that, denying ungodliness and worldly lusts, we should live soberly, righteously, and godly, in this present world." (Titus 2: 7-8; 11-12)

"He that walketh uprightly walketh surely: but he that perverteth his ways shall be known." (Proverbs 10: 9)

"A talebearer revealeth secrets: but he that is of a faithful spirit concealeth the matter." (Proverbs 11:13)

"Better *is* the poor that walketh in his uprightness, than *he that is* perverse *in his* ways, though he *be* rich." (Proverbs 28: 6)

"Be not deceived: evil communications corrupt good manners." (1 Corinthians 15: 33)

"Thy word *is* true *from* the beginning: and every one of thy righteous judgments *endureth* forever." (Psalm 119: 160)

"These *are* the things that ye shall do; Speak ye every man the truth to his neighbour; execute the judgment of truth and peace in your gates: And let none of you imagine evil in your hearts against his neighbour; and love no false oath:

for all these *are things* I hate, saith the LORD." (Zechariah 8: 16-17)

"Lie not one to another, seeing that ye have put off the old man with his deeds; And have put on the new *man*, which is renewed in knowledge after the image of him that created him." (Colossians 3: 9-10)

"Sanctify them through thy truth: thy word is truth." (John 17: 17)

Reflection(s): "Let it go!" Let nothing and no one get in the way of your march toward greater success, and always remain goal directed and focused on "winning the game". Make sure all the "dots connect" in a rational manner and avoid blockages of progress by others or yourself. In stressful, tense, and emotional situations, time to practice WWWST concepts by using your head, not your mouth until you calm down. Practice: "Let it go!"

Question: Whether to trust or decide not to trust others and whether to operate as trustworthy or not, and to what extent? These are questions we all routinely face in communication with others. It is not unusual for a person to want to trust others, especially among those who are often around in proximity -- friends and loved ones. There are times when the decision on whether a person can be trusted is based upon current circumstances or situations and other times when the determination is based upon multiple years of awareness. Once it is determined that a person is not to be trusted, that decision is exceedingly difficult to overcome, especially if the matter involves dishonesty.

It has been said that you should not trust anyone fully without question, or to trust only close family members and, even then, trust on a limited basis. At the least be careful to limit trust to those of whom you are convinced have earned your trust. Likewise, it is important that each of us is conscious about being trustworthy, within and across business and personal relationships. It is a choice. There are some very simple and doable traits that each of us can actively show: be honest and honorable all times; love one another as self and be willing to show it, noting that in love relationships each person is trustworthy and loyal; be integrous always; and think and do the right thing within and across all groups in communications.

Unfortunately, there are people who will routinely "smile in your face" and, later, demonstrate that those smiles were phony, at best, and at times they will take actions that turn out to be vengeful and hateful. They are quick to sabotage when out of site. It is better not to spend time trying to convince these types of people about right and wrong or to exert energy attempting to make them like or respect you. It is they who may or may not realize some day the value of trustworthiness, professionalism, honor, and friendship and not you; again, it is a choice one makes. Practice!

Reader - Think; Share; Reflect: _____

_____

- Weapons Free (compliant legally) - Think and do everything in your power to avoid a lifestyle of being around or using illegal weapons. There are rules for recreational hunting and self-defense which, when applied to specified situations, are acceptable in society. These rules do not fit in any way if the intent in possession or use of weapons may cause unprovoked harm to self or others. Think, plan, act responsibly by following the law and the standards for "doing unto others" what you would expect and desire, if you were confronted with the same situation. Practice!

  ➤ *Alignment with Bible Passages:*

  "No weapon that is formed against thee shall prosper; and every tongue *that* shall rise against thee in judgment thou shalt condemn. This is the heritage of the servants of the LORD, and their righteousness *is* of me, saith the LORD." (Isaiah 54: 17)

"Ye have heard that it hath been said, An eye for an eye, and a tooth for a tooth. But I say unto you, That ye resist not evil: but whosoever shall smite thee on thy right cheek, turn to him the other also." (Matthew 5: 38-39)

"Then said Jesus unto him, Put up again thy sword into his place: for all they that take the sword shall perish with the sword." (Matthew 26: 52)

"Finally, my brethren, be strong in the Lord, and in the power of his might. Put on the whole armor of God, that ye may be able to stand against the wiles of the devil. For we wrestle not against flesh and blood, but against principalities, against powers, against the rulers of the darkness of this world, against spiritual wickedness in high *places*." (Ephesians 6: 10-12)

"If it be possible, as much as lieth in you, live peaceably with all men. . . .

Be not overcome of evil, but overcome evil with good." (Romans 12: 18; 21)

"Be strong and courageous, be not afraid nor dismayed for the king of Assyria, nor for all the multitude that *is* with him: for *there be* more with us than with him: With him *is* an arm of flesh; but with us *is* the LORD our God to help us, and to fight our battles. And the people rested themselves upon the words of Hezekiah king of Judah." (2 Chronicles 32: 7-8)

"There is no king saved by the multitude of an host: a mighty man is not delivered by much strength. An horse *is* a vain thing for safety: neither shall he deliver *any* by his great strength. Behold, the eye of the LORD *is* upon them that fear him, upon them that hope in his mercy." (Psalm 33: 16-18)

"He delighteth not in the strength of the horse: he taketh not pleasure in the legs of a man. The LORD taketh pleasure in them that fear him, in those that hope in his mercy." (Psalm 147: 10-11)

"Then was Jesus led up of the Spirit into the wilderness to be tempted of the devil . . . And when the tempter came to him, he said, if thou be the Son of God, command that these stones be made bread. But he answered and said, It is written, Man shall not live by bread alone, but by every word that proceedeth out of the mouth of God." (Matthew 4: 1, 3-4)

"Then said David to the Philistine, Thou comest to me with a sword, and with a spear, and with a shield: but I come to thee in the name of the LORD of hosts, the God of the armies of Israel, whom thou hast defied." (1 Samuel 17: 45)

Reflection(s): "Let it go!" Let nothing and no one get in the way of your march toward greater success, and always remain goal directed and focused on "winning the game". Make sure all the "dots connect" in a rational manner and avoid blockages of progress by others or yourself. In stressful, tense, and emotional situations, time to practice WWWST concepts by using your head, not your mouth until you calm down. Practice: "Let it go!"

Always keep in mind the thought: "Leave other people alone except to help them!" Think about how many incidents and conflicts and violence could have been avoided if those involved had practiced this point: "Leave other people alone except to help them!" Mind your own business and stay out of the business of others is another way of putting it. Still another common and effective phrase is the following: Treat others as you wish to be treated. Some conflicts are unavoidable or, at the least, difficult to prevent. The better path toward resolution is to talk it out, including listening to the points of view of others and giving serious consideration to those ideas. Then use common sense in response and no weapons to resolve conflicts.

The possession of weapons may give a person a sense of comfort for prevention against harm. Also, weapons may be used in a reasonable manner for hunting. Weapons, however, should not be used in violence perpetrated upon another person or oneself. The use of a weapon is often a final act that cannot be reversed. In anger it is always better to walk away and cool off and not to attempt to resolve or address the problem at that exact time. It is really that simple; just walk away and deal with the situation later once you have had a chance to cool off. Too often it becomes a matter of pride and finding it important to demonstrate that you are not afraid, and you want to prove you will not be intimidated. No! Walk away rather than allow yourself to get caught in a situation where violence or serious argument will be the result of your communication. Likewise, there is no good time or reason to intimidate another person or to bully a person into submission as a means for resolving conflict. If you are a person who may tend to have a problem with quick anger and problems with patience, you should not carry weapons on your person or in a vehicle in which you are riding -- too easy to allow anger to overpower your sense of purpose and ability to avoid the temptation to use the weapon to settle your differences. No! Practice: "Let it go!"

Reader - Think; Share; Reflect: _____

_____

- (WWWST) What to say, when to say it and when to stop talking - In communication begin with and maintain a smile on your face throughout the conversation or presentation. Be factual, avoid speculation and always be honest and accurate in each comment made. It is best to avoid saying "no comment", as it may imply you are hiding something. No excuses or whining and do not seek pity, and never speak when angry. Calm down first and do not say what you are thinking if unhappy. It is important not to make comments about someone who is not present. If not well prepared for the subject, delay until another time or delegate the task of responding to someone else who may be better able to respond. If you do not know a good response, say that you do not know. When in doubt or when you have already sufficiently addressed the mission or topic, stop talking. Better not to say it if not sure whether you should. Again, keep smiling. Practice!

➢ *Alignment with Bible Passages:*

"And that ye study to be quiet, and to do your own business, and to work with your own hands, as we commanded you. That ye may walk honestly toward them that are without, and *that* ye may have lack of nothing." (1 Thessalonians 4: 11-12)

"And the same day, when the even was come, he saith unto them, Let us pass over unto the other side. And when they had sent away the multitude, they took him even as he was in the ship. And there were also with him other little ships. And there arose a great storm of wind, and the waves beat into the ship, so that it was now full. And he was in the hinder part of the ship, asleep on a pillow: and they awake him, and say unto him, Master, carest thou not that we perish? And he arose, and rebuked the wind, and said unto the sea, Peace, be still. And the wind ceased, and there was a great calm. And he said unto them, Why are ye so fearful? how is it that ye have no faith? (Mark 4: 35-40)

"Finally, brethren, farewell. Be perfect, be of good comfort, be of one mind, live in peace; and the God of love and peace shall be with you." (2 Corinthians: 13: 11)

"And say unto him, Take heed, and be quiet; fear not, neither be faint-hearted for the two tails of these smoking firebrands, for the fierce anger of Rezin with Syria, and of the son of Remaliah." (Isaiah 7: 4)

"A Soft answer turneth away wrath: but grievous words stir up anger." (Proverbs 15: 1)

"A wholesome tongue *is* a tree of life: but perverseness therein *is* a breach in the spirit . . . The lips of the wise disperse knowledge: but the heart of the foolish *doeth* not so." (Proverbs 15: 4; 7)

"Set a watch, O LORD, before my mouth; keep the door of my lips." (Psalm 141: 3)

"A time to rend, and a time to sew; a time to keep silence, and a time to speak." (Ecclesiastes 3: 7)

"Not that which goeth into the mouth defileth a man; but that which cometh out of the mouth, this defileth a man." (Matthew 15: 11)

"Wherefore, my beloved brethren, let every man be swift to hear, slow to speak, slow to wrath." (James 1: 19)

Reflection(s): "Let it go!" Let nothing and no one get in the way of your march toward greater success, and always remain goal directed and focused on "winning the game". Make sure all the "dots connect" in a rational manner and avoid blockages of progress by others or yourself. In stressful, tense, and emotional situations, time to practice WWWST concepts by using your head, not your mouth until you calm down. Practice: "Let it go!"

The bottom line is thinking before you speak and determining prior to speaking whether the comment adds value to the conversation or not. It matters in every conversation what you say, when to say it and when it is better to hold on to the comment and leave it unspoken. Far too often people tend to operate otherwise and speak without thinking and say too much -- too late! Stop it; better for us to practice listening more and talking less.

A few examples follow -- still long way to go for needed changes and growth in the attitudes of people. One very clear example of how important it is to think before you comment is the situation in the year 2018 which resulted in the resignation of a Texas superintendent, following his "posting" on Facebook a response to an online newspaper story where he was critical of the quarterback of the Houston Texans football team, stating among other things, "You can't count on a black quarterback." He resigned, expressing in his resignation letter his deepest apologies for making such a comment -- too late! He also stated that the comments were wrong and inappropriate. So true. He apologized directly to the quarterback for his remarks in a public statement, and he expressed appreciation to the quarterback for not criticizing or belittling him for his remarks, choosing instead peace and positivity. Of course, beyond the mistake of making the original, offensive public statement of this nature, also troubling was the attitude and ignorance displayed, especially by an educator in a position of leadership. This incident could easily have been avoided by thinking before acting about "what to say, when to say it and when to stop talking".

Another situation involved a radio host in 2007 in a program simulcast on a television station, where the host made the comment to look at those "nappy-headed hos" (whores) in referring to a very talented, successful women's basketball team. The comment was made after another radio personality called the team "hardcore hos" (whores). The show was cancelled shortly following the program. A Georgia superintendent faced discipline and later resigned in 2018 following release of an audio recording filled with racist rants, including use of the term "nigger" and other derogatory comments about construction workers. Another case where attitude matters and demonstration of why it is better to think before speaking and to know what to say, when to say it and when to stop talking.

Still another example of a person speaking before thinking involved the general manager of a major league baseball team in 1987, where during a public television interview in responding to a question about why there are not more black baseball managers, he stated that "I truly believe that they may not have some of the necessities to be, let's say, a field manager, or perhaps a general manager." The interview host asked whether he really believed that, and the general manager stated, "Well, I don't say that all of them, but they certainly are short. How many quarterbacks do you have? How many pitchers do you have that are black?" And, he went on to say that black athletes are not good swimmers because they do not have the buoyancy... and more. Stop it; stop talking if not appropriate and helpful to self or others. In the year 2020 many of the residents and students in a school district in the state of Texas were embarrassed following a ruling by the school principal (and supported by the central administration) that a senior high school student of color was required to get a haircut because of the length of his hair and the dreadlocks style. The student was suspended and told that if he did not cut his hair, he would not be allowed to participate in the senior prom or graduation ceremony. The story was reported on national news amid complaints from the family that the decision was discriminatory, as the hair style was part of his family heritage and noting that the student had attended the school for several years without problems and had made good grades. The story was broadcast nationally. Due to national attention and strong disagreement with the ruling, the student received a large scholarship from a celebrity and attended the 92nd Academy Awards show in California as guests of the producers of an Oscar nominated short film about hair. The school district's reactions to the situation came across as arrogant, insensitive and tone deaf as well as backwards, especially given the diverse composition of the student body and criticisms by students not of color that they had not faced the same consequences. The student decided to transfer to a different school district. Those involved in handling the situation could have benefited by paying more attention to what to say, when to say it and when to stop talking.

It is quite common, and we can all recall instances where we wished the person talking would stop. Whether such occurrences involved a formal presentation or casual conversation, church sermon, school speech, television or radio interview or report, or business meeting, in these moments it may seem that the end of the talk is long awaited by all. We routinely forget or ignore the common rules of speaking, for example:

- Think before speaking.
- Make the point succinctly, then pause.

- Connect the sentences in a paragraph and include a topic, middle substance and ending.
- Know the facts and, in general, what you are speaking about before you open your mouth.
- Never speak when angry and show no frowning in public.
- Know your audience and communicate with them, not to them.
- Do not complain about someone who is not in the conversation.
- Listen. Stop talking.

I have developed a routine that if I stop listening before you stop talking, I will disengage and move away from the presentation or conversation. Otherwise it turns into a distraction, and no one wishes to experience distraction by choice. I choose not to be bored or distracted, for sure. Among the many challenges during doctoral studies at The University of Texas at Austin, one of the intriguing exercises was to make presentations within a brief, designated period, ten minutes or so to make your case. Yet, it was a highly effective practice for polishing our skills for making effective presentations. Practice!

Reader - Think; Share; Reflect – think of other examples of helpful tips on what to say, when to say it, and when to stop talking.

_____

_____

- Zero bullying (allowed, initiated, or involvement and no fighting) - Treat everyone as you wish to be treated every day, period! Better to forgive and forget than to retaliate or get even. No time to hold grudges and no victory in overpowering or deliberately being mean to another person. Practice the skills for learning from the past, enjoying the present and looking forward to the future. Learn the skills for forgiving. "Hanging on" to the past is a waste of time and helps no one, including you. Anger is an emotion which can be controlled, remembering if they anger you by the things they say or do, they have "conquered" you. Practice!

> *Alignment with Bible Passages:*

"Thou shalt not avenge, nor bear any grudge against the children of thy people, but thou shalt love thy neighbour as thyself: I *am* the LORD." (Leviticus 19: 18)

"FRET not thyself because of evildoers, neither be thou envious against workers of iniquity. For they shall soon be cut down like the grass, and wither as the green herb. Trust in the LORD, and do good; *so* shalt thou dwell in the land, and verily thou shalt be fed. Delight thyself also in the LORD; and he shall give thee the desires of thine heart . . . Cease from anger, and forsake wrath: fret not thyself in any wise to do evil. For evildoers shall be cut off: but those that wait upon the LORD, they shall inherit the earth." (Psalm 37: 1-4; 8-9)

"Recompense to no man evil for evil. Provide things honest in the sight of all men. If it be possible, as much as lieth in you, live peaceably with all men." (Romans 12: 17-18)

"These six *things* doth the LORD hate; yea, seven *are* an abomination unto him. A proud look, a lying tongue, and hands that shed innocent blood, An heart that deviseth wicked imaginations, feet that be swift in running to mischief, A false witness *that* speaketh lies, and he that soweth discord among brethren." (Proverbs 6: 16 – 19)

"A soft answer turneth away wrath: but grievous words stir up anger." (Proverbs 15: 1)

"Whoso rewardeth evil for good, evil shall not depart from his house. The beginning of strife *is as* when one letteth out water: therefore leave off contention, before it be meddled with." (Proverbs 17: 13-14)

"Ye have heard that it hath been said, Thou shalt love thy neighbour, and hate thine enemy. But I say unto you, Love your enemies, bless them that curse you, do good to them that hate you, and pray for them which despitefully use you, and persecute you; That ye may be the children of your Father which is in heaven: for he maketh his sun to rise on the evil and on the good, and sendeth rain on the just and on the unjust. For if ye love them which love you, what reward have ye? Do not even the publicans the same? And if ye salute your brethren only, what do ye more than others? Do not even the publicans so? Be ye therefore perfect, even as your Father which is in heaven is perfect." (Matthew 5: 43-48)

"The golden rule. Therefore all things whatsoever ye would that men should do to you, do ye even so to them: for this is the law and the prophets." (Matthew 7: 12)

"Let no corrupt communication proceed out of your mouth, but that which is good to the use of edifying, that it may minister grace unto the hearers." (Ephesians 4: 29)

"And thou shalt love the LORD thy God with all thy heart, and with all thy soul, and with all thy mind, and with all thy strength: this *is* the first commandment. And the second *is* like, *namely* this, Thou shalt love thy neighbour as thyself. There is none other commandment greater than these." (Mark 12: 30-31)

Reflection(s): "Let it go!" Let nothing and no one get in the way of your march toward greater success, and always remain goal directed and focused on "winning the game". Make sure all the "dots connect" in a rational manner and avoid blockages of progress by others or yourself. In stressful, tense, and emotional situations, time to practice WWWST concepts by using your head, not your mouth until you calm down. Practice: "Let it go!"

There is no good reason to bully or intimidate another person. Everyone deserves to live in peace and freedom from harm, verbal and physical. It is not only important not to bully or harm, it is important that each one of us reaches out to help others, as a high priority. With wide use of social media, bullying is more prevalent than before. Such cowardly behavior can be perpetrated from afar but is still just as hurtful and harmful.

I am proud of and thankful for the lessons learned in growing up, especially at home. My parents were consistent and repetitive in reminding my brothers and sisters and me during childhood and beyond that we should always help and not harm other people. Those lessons were consistently promoted in the neighborhood among our adult neighbors, teachers, and ministers.

There are circumstances where those you may wish to assist would rather go it alone. That is, the act of reaching out to help others is only appreciated as helpful when it is welcomed by the recipient of such offers. And, again, the act of bullying another person may come across as verbal – or non-verbal (appearance of ignoring a person), and it may be physical. A person should not push themselves upon others, even in offers to be helpful.

I can recall numerous instances while growing up as a child and in adulthood, observing comments and acts of kindness. I have also observed the opposite, including conduct, which was unwelcomed, crude, and disrespectful of others and bullying. Fortunately, the acts of kindness in my experience and observations far exceed that of any other conduct. In fact, I am proud of and thankful for having the attitude of gaining joy and happiness when I observe others enjoying happiness and joy -- it can be infectious, indeed.

And always keep in mind the thought: "Leave other people alone!" Practice!

Reader - Think; Share; Reflect: _____

_____

What To Say And When To Stop Talking

Common Sense
Continuous Improvement
Discipline
Focus
Follow Law
Healthy Lifestyle
Honesty
Honor
Listening
Love
Loyalty
Protect Property
Reading
Respect
Right Way
Space
Teamwork
Trustworthiness
Weapons Free
Zero Bullying

Logo - Author and Mary (Brown) Ruegg;
Chart - Darchase Designs

WINNERS ALWAYS PRACTICE PROGRAM (WAPP)

Twenty-one easy-to-address behaviors, practices, qualities and areas of growth and development to win -- in games and life. By practicing all day everyday each of these categories, the chances to win increases in all phases of life, games, school and for getting along with others within and across race, class and otherwise. Yes, we can all succeed and get along with others if we want to and practice toward perfection in the following, well established and accepted behaviors, and practices, as provided not including biblical alignments and reflections and reflections:

1. Common sense -- Common sense relates to natural tendencies and knowledge based upon routine growth experiences. The information "bank" to "pull from" or benefit from is common to all, and special training and experiences are not required for reference in determining how best to behave. Or, stated in more common terms, act like you are smart or well trained and dignified, especially, if others are around or may be affected by your behavior. Always avoid behaving "stupidly" when it is just as easy to behave "smartly." Practice!

2. Continuous improvement - No one is perfect, and everyone can and should strive to improve. Part of the human growth and development experience is that natural changes occur over which we have no control. Regarding those things over which we do have control, it is imperative to plan for and take advantage of opportunities to improve, within and across all forms of knowledge and conduct. It is safe to say that a person is on the incline in growth and development or in decline, as nothing in the human existence remains the same, over time. Never, ever give up or quit. Practice!

3. Discipline - Self-discipline is about making choices that are controlled by only one person, that is you! It is one of the most important decisions and, yet, too often one of the most challenging to manage. When managed effectively you stay out of trouble and avoid being confronted with problems and

circumstances which can easily become a distraction and block progress toward happiness and well-being. Practice!

4. Focus - It is so easy to set goals and, yet, much more difficult to focus and set plans for and take the actions that are necessary to achieve them. Focusing entails controlling thoughts and actions to address with laser like attention on what matters the most. To focus is also not allowing distractions that may delay or prevent the outcomes desired. You can always find some reason not to focus and many better reasons to focus and maintain it, regardless of the temptations to do otherwise. Practice!

5. Follow Law - Laws exist for a reason: to protect all from harm, promote democracy and support us all as we seek to enjoy the "common good" and better quality of life. Do what you are supposed to do and not what you are not. Always keep the brain "open", and keep the thoughts and actions directed toward advantages for and reasons to follow all laws whether local, state or nationally generated. There is always a possibility of being caught, thereby, bringing negative attention toward you and penalties which can derail or ruin the "road" to winning on and off the playing field or court. Remember, in the "world" of current technology, officials can find out all kinds of information through review of records from cameras, cell phones, credit cards and banking records. Sooner or later when you fail to follow the law, you will be caught and will face the consequences of your actions. Practice!

6. Healthy lifestyle (no alcohol, drugs, eat right & exercise) - Being healthy is directly affected and driven by lifestyle and choices about eating, drinking, exercising, resting, and intake of substances. Attitude makes a difference realizing, for example, that expending the energy for a smile is far less difficult to develop than to develop a frown, and the impact is more healthful. To smile and seek happiness and acting out such an emotion is a good idea. Remember, how you live your life is your decision and none is more important than to choose to live a healthy lifestyle. Practice!

7. Honor (think and act your best with integrity and character) – Everyone has a name. That "good" name represents your family, self, and history -- past and future. The best way to protect that "good" name is to think and act with integrity and strong character. Such behavior is expected and preferred in all circles of life across the world, characterized by carrying oneself and treating others with respect and dignity and in accordance with the law and "high" moral character. Practice!

8. Honesty - Tell the truth and think, act, and live truthfully in all communications and transactions. Honesty is important whether related to the commission or omission of actions or comments in pursuance of the truth. Even in cases where the truth is not apparent or may be hidden from open view or misunderstood, the best approach is to "fill in the blanks" for accuracy rather than to allow misperceptions or lack of access to truth to prevail. Practice!

9. Listening -. To listen is a major component in communication and is as important as speaking. There is a major difference in hearing and listening. Hearing simply perceives the sounds, while listening requires hearing the sounds and applying what is heard to a sense of meaning and determining an appropriate response, if any. Hearing is a natural function of the body in acknowledgement of sound; listening requires thinking and action. Practice!

10. Love (give and seek over hatred) - To love and be loved are equally important and a significant part of enjoying a successful lifestyle. Love, in a real sense, is connected within and across every emotion, thought and action; although, you cannot see it and touch it. It is always there. Each one of us wants to be loved and appreciated, and each one of us has the innate ability to give and receive love. There is no room or good time in a "high quality" lifestyle for hatred, either to spread, devote time to it in thoughts or actions, or to experience it. Practice!

11. Loyalty - Loyalty is an important factor for achieving a common goal. Once the members of the group are identified and the group norms are established, there is an expectation of loyalty or

agreement with all members of the team or group. Membership will change over time, with new members added and others leaving the group. Once norms are clear and established and there is a goal in mind for winning or high achievement, everyone has to believe in and practice the concept of counting on other members of the group and being counted upon, as a loyal or committed member of the group. Practice!

12. Protect property (of self and others and not steal) - It is not complicated. There is no good reason to steal or even think about it. Besides being the wrong thing to do by law and violation in morality, stealing is hurtful to both self and others. It does not matter that no one is around to see you steal; it is just as wrong. At the same time, it is important to plan for and take actions to protect one's own property. Take steps even as simple as keeping keys or wallet in the same, exact place while traveling or sleeping or locking the door behind you for safety and protection of property. Think, plan, practice!

13. Reading - Reading is basic to all other knowledge, and it is key to all learning and the "spine" which holds everything together. If you cannot read, everybody will know it. Also, there is no "victory" in being illiterate. When you speak, your speech is a clear and public indicator of your level of preparation and intelligence. Reading is a means to acquire communication skills. A person who is a poor or reluctant reader shows his or her lack of preparation and obvious unwillingness to grow in the skill set required for a good fit in society. You have a choice whether to be viewed as intelligent or unintelligent and, like any other skill set, you must practice each day to improve. Practice!

14. Respect (self and others and mind your business) - You deserve to be respected and so does everyone else. Respect starts with self and how you think and act and is apparent in all you say and do. It is far better to demonstrate positive regard toward others than to leave interpretation of your intent to chance. It is also important to give and receive respectful gestures and non-verbal cues in communication with other people. When confronted with decisions on whether to get involved or not, better to mind

your own business, especially if the issue is not of your direct concern. Stay out of it. Practice!

15. Right way (over wrong) - It is not complicated. Do the right thing, regardless of the circumstances or what may appear to be a possible advantage to do otherwise. Doing the right thing enables you to enjoy the available benefits, while doing the wrong thing works in the opposite direction, short or long term. The decision to do right or wrong starts internally. If you must think about it, whether the action is right or wrong, always, always choose to do the "right" thing over wrong. The self-monitoring mechanisms inside should guide you in the right direction, with heavy reliance upon past experiences and an internal knowledge base in place to guide you. Practice!

16. Space (give, protect, stay in your lane) - It is most difficult to accurately determine whether someone wants or does not want a person in their "space" or near them. Better to "play it safe" and always be mindful that personal space is deserved by everyone, and a violation of that privilege can often cause discomfort for them and you. Make sure you are "invited" in proximity, with no exceptions of leaving it to chance or guessing, if okay. If not clear of an invitation into another person's "space", keep a safe distance away from him or her. And if you believe your private space is being violated, quietly move away to create a greater distance away from you, or simply inform the other person of your feeling of discomfort. Practice!

17. Teamwork (over self)—The concept of placing team or common good over self is one of the most cherished notions across the world. It is what is being practiced when, as a nation or church group or athletic team or any similar organization, the preferred standard is what is good for one is good for all. It has been said that "you cannot be almost on the team". You are on the team and act as such, or you are not really a full member of the group. Placing team over self is one of the most important principles of team sports and winning the game. It is also part of what drives the laws we live by and other rules which govern the common good. Practice!

18. Trustworthiness (trust, trusted) - The principle of trustworthiness is simple to understand but difficult for some to follow, either to trust or be trusted. When a person shares information or receives it, better that it remains among those who are directly engaged in the communication, written or verbal form. Whether the communication occurs among those in a small group of two or many more, it is important to practice the skills for trusting and being trustworthy.

19. Weapons Free (compliant legally) - Think and do everything in your power to avoid a lifestyle of being around or using illegal weapons. There are rules for recreational hunting and self-defense which, when applied to specified situations, are acceptable in society. These rules do not fit in any way if the intent in possession or use of weapons may cause unprovoked harm to self or others. Think, plan, act responsibly by following the law and the standards for "doing unto others" what you would expect and desire, if you were confronted with the same situation. Practice!

20. (WWWST) What to say, when to say it and when to stop talking - In communication begin with and maintain a smile on your face throughout the conversation or presentation. Be factual, avoid speculation and always be honest and accurate in each comment made. It is best to avoid saying "no comment", as it may imply you are hiding something. No excuses or whining and do not seek pity, and never speak when angry. Calm down first and do not say what you are thinking if unhappy. It is important not to make comments about someone who is not present. If not well prepared for the subject, delay until another time or delegate the task of responding to someone else who may be better able to respond. If you do not know a good response, say that you do not know. When in doubt or when you have already sufficiently addressed the mission or topic, stop talking. Better not to say it if not sure whether you should. And, again, keep smiling. Practice!

21. Zero bullying (allowed, initiated, or involvement and no fighting) - Treat everyone as you wish to be treated every day,

period! Better to forgive and forget than to retaliate or get even. No time to hold grudges and no victory in overpowering or deliberately being mean to another person. Practice the skills for learning from the past, enjoying the present and looking forward to the future. Learn the skills for forgiving. "Hanging on" to the past is a waste of time and helps no one, including you. Anger is an emotion which can be controlled, remembering if they anger you by the things they say or do, they have "conquered" you. Practice!

— Chapter Ten —

Thinking Strategically for Better Schools and School Districts, Business Organizations

PART I. Strategic Thinking - Ideas on School Improvement: What to Do to Ensure Success in Schools and Businesses

9 "PLUS 1" KEYS to VICTORY FOR BUSINESS and SCHOOL ORGANIZATIONS

In this chapter there is discussion of nine ideas to apply for success in businesses and schools and a category termed "plus one" which is to be applied separately to businesses and schools. These two organizations are more similar than dissimilar in leadership as required for excellence in performance and success overall.

1. <u>Time on task protected and monitored</u> - Every minute is important in the school or business day and week. It is important to have a system in place to routinely monitor and ensure that time is devoted to student learning each hour, day, week.

2. <u>Decisions based upon data and intended outcomes</u> - The data are readily available across all aspects of preparation and results. The only way to plan successfully is to base decisions upon the data.

3. <u>Actions based upon mission and policies</u> - Plan with the intent to act then act based upon the mission and policies of the organization. To act without planning is foolish and often requires re-calculations and you lose the opportunity to measure progress.

4. <u>Communication respectful and positive</u> – Treat everyone as a person of value and with respect and dignity. Excellence in communication requires listening by all parties, and the points of view of each person must be given positive regard and consideration.

5. <u>Customer service emphasized</u> – Always work at providing the absolute best service possible each moment of every day, while remaining focused on accomplishing the mission and goals of the organization. Treat customers as you want to be treated.

6. <u>Growth and development required</u> – We can all grow and improve our knowledge and skills. Plan with the "end in mind" and practice continuously with intent to reach an extraordinary level of expertise for successful outcomes in delivery of service.

7. <u>Teamwork stressed</u> – The greater good is accomplished through teamwork over what is done by individuals. It is important that each person in the organization is shown respect with the expectation of the same being demonstrated in return. Treat each person as a champion with whom you share a common goal of "winning" the game or success on the task.

8. <u>Expectations high and all held accountable for results</u> – All deserve to be respected and considered as capable of achieving at the same level of expectations. Do not allow "opt outs" or failure to try in any organization. Focus attention on outcomes over process, and never confuse effort with accuracy or mastery. All who are involved in the process, customers and service deliverers must play their roles in the best possible way.

9. <u>Victories celebrated</u> – It is important to set benchmarks for achievement, and when reached to take the time to celebrate. Continue to move the "bar" higher and higher, so that the improvement is continuous, and the organization does not become stagnant or complacent. The moment at which you fail to improve is the moment you begin to move into decline in the organization.

All the nine points above relate to school and business operations. The information which follows relates more specifically to either schools or businesses, as categorized:

Plus One Zone - Schools: a) A high quality teacher in every classroom; b) every employee expected to support reading and writing instruction in pursuit of a culture of excellence in literacy; c) resources aligned with and organizational structure designed to support the teacher-student relationship; d) curriculum management principles emphasized; e) positive parent and community partnerships promoted; f) practice of staying in your lane approach for all concerned; g) focus is on teaching more; drilling and testing less!!!

Plus One Zone – Businesses: a) Every employee held responsible for knowing and valuing the business; b) high knowledge of craft at each position; c) business management principles emphasized; d) positive business and community partnerships promoted; e) no excuses; f) practice of staying in your lane approach for all concerned; g) focus is on people, not things.

Part II. Strategic Thinking Continued - Ideas on School Improvement: What to Do to Ensure Success in Schools and Businesses

CRITICAL ISSUES in REFORM and CHANGE for IMPROVEMENT

The ideas which follow are important considerations for addressing the support and services needed for schools and school districts to improve student learning, with particular emphasis on putting conditions in place for all children to be successful in learning -- "all means all"!

A. Standards and expectations are in place and high for students and employees.

B. An action plan is in place and rational for student learning success.

C. The schools/districts are organized for results.

D. The focus is always on children first.

E. Goals, objectives, and indicators of success are established for the district and schools.

F. Resources are aligned with the education plan to best support teaching and learning.

G. Each classroom has a highly qualified and certified teacher.

H. Growth, development, evaluation, and accountability plans are in place for all instructional personnel.

I. The environment is proper for teaching and learning

J. Diversity is celebrated and all students and personnel are treated with respect and appreciation.

K. Decision making is data based and supported by current research.

L. Leadership is focused on what matters the most: student success and well-being.

Part III. Strategic Thinking Continued - Ideas on School Improvement: What to Do to Ensure Success in Schools

AREAS of FOCUS TO MAKE the GREATEST DIFFERENCE in GOVERNANCE, LEADERSHIP, and MORE

Support for school boards, superintendents, principals, teachers, and administrative support for staff. The following information identifies concepts and areas of concern that require attention and plans for achieving results in the reform movement. It is highly recommended that current and aspiring leaders consider utilization of these concepts and ideas as guides toward accomplishing their visions of effective leadership. This section includes a compilation of ideas and principles of leadership gathered from multiple sources over several years of observations and interactions with authors and others who share the same or similar beliefs. The insights gained from the colleagues and authors named in the acknowledgements section of the book have been invaluable in shaping the ideas about successful leadership that are presented here. Organizations such as the Alabama Association of School Boards, American Association of School Administrators, American Educational Research Association, Georgia Association of Educational Leaders, Phi Delta Kappa International, Texas Association of School Boards, Texas Association of Secondary School Principals, Texas Elementary Principals and Supervisors Association, and others have been both beneficial and appreciated. The key principles for consideration are as follows:

A. Excellence in leadership for desired results - Leadership makes such an important difference, it cannot be left to chance who assumes or maintains such roles. Put measures in place for selection and routine review of the success of the leader, based on data -- not to be left to "chance".

B. Address issues of excellence, adequacy, and equity in education – Follow research reports and monitor the available data, routinely, and take appropriate actions based upon such data to assure excellence in achievement, equity and adequacy in distribution of resources and assignment to courses and staff being held accountable for results. Plan distribution of resources and assignment to courses in a fair, rational, and intentional manner, based upon the needs of children.

C. Roles and responsibilities for school board members, superintendents, principals, and other leaders in education – Follow the law and district policies on roles and responsibilities and practice how best to operate as a team. Generally, the role of school board members is to set policies, and the administration is responsible for implementing the policies adopted; yet, there are "grey" areas of mutual responsibilities. Positive communication and respect among all concerned are required factors for assuring maximum results and positive movement toward the mission of the school system.

D. Governance, ethics, and politics of education – School system governance is the provision of oversight and adoption of policies for mission, vision, controls, direction, and accountability in the organization. Ethics in schools and businesses relate to doing the "right thing" and doing so at the "right time" in the "right way". Education is provided in a political environment and, yet, all decisions must be made in accordance with what is best for the children and never putting the "politics" first.

E. Policy development, implementation, and evaluation – Consider important factors such as need and purpose of the policy and the implications and effect on all concerned in implementation. Determine evaluation standards as part of the development procedure in assessing the extent to which desired outcomes are realized.

F. Balanced, comprehensive approach in teaching children how to read – Plan prior to introduction and throughout program for ensuring effective reading instruction. Take the time to determine short-term and long-term effects of actions taken during the teaching and learning process. Routinely hold Professional Learning Community (PLC) meetings, including teachers, counselors, librarians, and administrators for review of data, progress in achieving learning objectives and patterns on effect of strategies in teaching various lessons. Require that faculty and staff and children read each day!

G. Support for teachers of children with special needs – Show respect for all personnel and children involved in or affected by special circumstances. Treat each teacher and child as a champion with whom you share a common goal of successful outcomes. Show respect to all and expect to be respected in return.

H. Excellence in customer service – Hold high expectations for all on positive communication, with special emphasis on development of and practicing the skills for listening. Listen more than you talk and show genuine interest in what you hear. Treat customers better than you would, reasonably, expect to be treated and work at solving problems rather than creating or allowing new ones.

I.   Personnel management & accountability – Ensure that policies are in place, shared widely and followed fairly and equitably, regarding personnel management. Hold all employees accountable based upon written policies, procedures, and targets for expected outcomes. Make it clear from the start the rewards for success and consequences for not achieving expectations.

J.   School-site management and focus inside schools – Maintain laser level focus on what matters most, that is, what goes on and has impact on children and employees inside the school. Encourage those most affected by decisions or circumstances to be involved in the decision-making process. Have confidence in parents, community, personnel, and children and operate with the understanding that those inside the schools know what is best for them.

K.   School environment - facilities clean and attractive; dress code implementation; reducing the drop-out rate and increasing the attendance rate; rules are monitored and discipline imposed fairly; positive communication between adults and children and more – what things look like matters; so does it matter to demonstrate to youth and employees exposure to positive things over negative. Establish procedures to test whether the environment is suitable for instruction and adjust as needed for improvements, always with consideration of short and long-term impact of the change.

L.   Parental and community engagement for school and system success— "It takes the 'whole' village". Engage parents and community in a positive manner in the school environment. Such engagement includes conversations and completion of projects with common goals and activities in mind. Children perform better, and achievement is higher when parents and community are involved.

M. Celebration and awards – Take time to evaluate progress and show gratitude for work well done. Employees and all stakeholders in an organization appreciate being recognized and sharing in events that foster positive thinking regarding tasks completed and work accomplished.

Publications/Papers

- Brown, J. (1991). <u>Leader behavior and school effectiveness.</u> Ann Arbor: University Microfilms International (U.M.I.). Dissertation – <u>Leader behavior and school effectiveness.</u> Focus on a) site management and b) principals' leadership relative to instruction and home-school relations.
- Encyclopedia Article: Akins, W., & Brown, J. (1993). Sweatt v. Painter (1950) In Anderson, D., Asbury, C., Jones-Wilson, F., & Okazawa-Rey (Eds.). <u>The Encyclopedia of African American Education</u>.
- Brown, J. (1991). <u>Leader behavior and school effectiveness</u>. Paper presented at the annual meeting of the American Educational Research Association in Chicago, Illinois. Unpublished paper based upon research findings.

Web site: www.jcbil.com
Twitter: @jbrowneducator
www.facebook.com/johnny.e.brown.7/

Logo for Johnny & Carolyn Brown Institute for Learning

LOGO FOR WAPP – Author & Mary (Brown) Ruegg

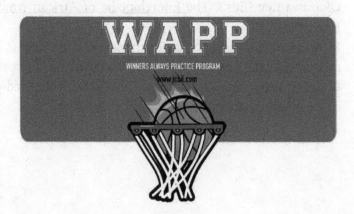